Wine by Style

Wine by Style

A practical guide to choosing wine by flavour, weight and colour

Fiona Beckett

Mitchell Beazley

Wine by Style by Fiona Beckett

First published in Great Britain in 1998 by Mitchell Beazley, an imprint of Reed Consumer Books
Limited, 25 Victoria Street, London SW1H 0EX and Auckland and Melbourne

A CIP catalogue record of this book is available from the British Library

ISBN 1 84000 030 9

Commissioning Editor: Sue Jamieson
Executive Art Editor: Fiona Knowles
Editor: Lucy Bridgers
Design: Geoff Fennell
Specially commissioned photography: Steven Morris
Production: Rachel Lynch, Ann Childers
Picture Research: Anna Kobryn
Index: Angie Hipkin

Typeset in Foundry

Printed and bound by Toppan Printing Company, China

CONTENTS

INTRODUCTION

When you first start drinking and buying wine it can be a bewildering experience – a world that everybody seems to know more about than you. There are so many wines, so many confusing and unfamiliar names that it seems an impossible task to get to grips with them all.

Gradually, as you try out different wines, you will find a few that you really enjoy. In sheer relief you may be tempted to buy them again and again. Then it's all to easy to get stuck in a rut, often paying more than you need for a wine that has ceased to be good value.

Wine by Style is all about giving you the confidence to take your acquaintanceship with wine a step further by helping you to identify the style of wine you enjoy. It takes a radically different approach to many wine books. Instead of looking in depth at the various wine producing regions of the world (an exercise you may well want to pursue at some point, but which can be daunting when you're starting out), I've concentrated on certain easily recognisable wine styles with which you're probably already familiar. Once you find a wine you consistently enjoy, all you have to do is to check out which other wines are made in the same style.

There's an important point to underline at this stage. People sometimes worry that if they prefer, say, a flowery German white to a claret, that there is something to be apologetic about, but there isn't a "right" and a "wrong" style of wine. You only have to think how tastes differ with respect to food. Some people are sweet-toothed, some are not. Some love to eat salads, others avoid them. People's tolerance of spicy food varies hugely. It would be surprising (and very dull) if we all liked the same wines.

What may happen is that your tastes will change. When you start drinking you may well be more attracted to a fresh, fruity white wine than a full-bodied red. Later you prefer wines with a stronger, more intense flavour. This is absolutely normal. If you draw a parallel with coffee, people very rarely start off with a double espresso. They take it with milk and two lumps of sugar and only gradually move on to stronger blends.

There's unlikely therefore to be just one style of wine that will suit you. It may change at different stages in your life. When you first start drinking wine in your twenties or thirties, you may be attracted by simple fruit flavours. Twenty years on when you've had a chance to taste a much wider range of wines, you may look for wines of greater maturity, subtlety and complexity. You can get bored with a style of wine like heavily oaked Chardonnay and start to look for something different. And, of course, wines themselves change. Choosing a lush, fruity New World Grenache or Malbec wasn't an option 10 or 15 years ago because the wines simply weren't available.

Your choice of wine may also change with your mood or the time of year. The fresh, crisp rosé you enjoyed so much on holiday is not necessarily going to be as appealing in the middle of winter when there's five degrees of frost outside. Similarly, a big gutsy red will just seem too heavy when it's warm and summery. And if you want to celebrate, you're far more likely to crack open a bottle of champagne or sparkling wine to mark the occasion than a dry white wine.

Which style of wine you pick also depends on the type of food you're eating – and who you're eating it with. As you can see from the Wine and Food section at the back of the book (pages 104–109), certain styles of wine suit certain foods. A light, crisp white wine, for example, would be overwhelmed by a rich, intensely flavoured beef dish, so, even if it is normally the kind of wine you prefer, you would probably be looking for a full-bodied red to match it.

Equally, you may want to take account of the likely preferences of your guests. More individual wines like aromatic whites and aged red wines and rarities are not to everyone's taste. If you have guests whose taste in wine you're uncertain about, you're more likely to be searching in the smooth, medium-bodied white and red sections.

It may also surprise you to learn that how you treat a bottle of wine (how long you keep it and the temperature at which you serve it, for instance) can affect its style, so I have included a section on how to store and serve wine and even how to recognise wine faults.

All this is not to replace one daunting set of rules with another – more an invitation to roam freely through the book and not to rule out certain styles of wine. Wine drinking should be a pleasure, not a trial. I hope this book brings that experience one step nearer for you.

WHAT INFLUENCES STYLE AND FLAVOUR?

At one time the style of wine produced by winemakers wasn't really a conscious decision. If they were working within the framework of rules that applied to the vineyards in their area, as most producers did, in countries such as France and Italy there was little choice about the varieties they could plant, when to harvest them or how many grapes the vines produced. Then, even more than now, they were at the mercy of the weather. If the vineyards were hit by frost there was little to be done about it. If it was sweltering hot when the time came to make the wine, it was hard to keep the temperature in the winery under control.

Now the situation is totally different. In many parts of the world, particularly in the newer winemaking countries of Australia, Chile, South Africa and New Zealand, that rigid framework of rules does not exist. Within the constraints of their resources, equipment and manpower, winemakers can do as they like. The huge hi-tech wineries of today can fashion more or less any kind of wine the market wants.

The most influential people are no longer the bureaucrats who administer the rules, but the buyers for large supermarket chains. How healthy this is debatable. There is justifiable concern about the extent to which the individuality of different wine producing regions is being lost and how wines are beginning to taste the same whichever part of the world they come from. Yet it can't be denied that the general standard of wine is higher than it has ever been.

Fortunately for all the technical progress that has occurred, the fact remains that wine is an agricultural crop and that the most important influence on style remains the type of grape that it made from and the climate in which it is grown. These and other influences are explored over the next few pages.

Grape varieties

The importance of the grape or grapes a wine is made from is recognised by the fact that the wines familiar to the greatest number of wine drinkers are varietals – wines named after grape varieties like Chardonnay and Cabernet Sauvignon. These are called "noble" grapes because of the fact that they are used to make some of the world's greatest wines, but increasing attention is being focused on lesser-known grapes which can offer new and different flavours. You can expect over the next few years to see more of obscure varieties such as Bonarda, Bouschet, Carmenère, César, Garganega and Grechetto.

Climate and soil

The French concept of *terroir* (the unique combination of climate, soil and situation) is now recognised throughout the world as increasingly important to the production of quality wines. New World winemakers may have once believed that they could achieve anything in the winery, but increasingly they have come to recognise the importance of picking sites best suited to the grape variety they want to plant.

Winemaking techniques

The advances in winemaking techniques, particularly temperature control and the use of cultured yeasts, have revolutionised the production of cheaper wines, making it possible to produce fresh, clean, characterful wines out of what even ten years ago would have been unpromising raw materials. The palate of flavours available to the modern winemaker is more sophisticated than it has ever been.

Oak

Not all wines, of course, are oaked, but the varied influence of different kinds of barrels can be quite dramatic. Oak can be an obvious influence or a subtle one, depending on the effect the winemaker is striving for. In general, the presence of oak will result in a fuller-bodied style of wine, though the use of oak chips can be used to round out the flavour.

How all these variables interact and come together in a finished wine is a fascinating process. The next few pages explore these influences further.

GRAPE VARIETIES

It is the grape variety or blend of varieties it is made from that gives a wine its defining character. That might seem obvious. You can hardly, after all, make a red wine out of white grapes (although winemakers do occasionally make white out of red), but it amounts to more than that. Regardless of climate, regardless of modern techniques, if you harvest a crop of, for example, Chardonnay, you know you're not going to end up with a wine that smells of grass or gooseberries.

Of course this is truer of some grapes than of others. You're unlikely to taste a dry Italian white and say "Aha, Trebbiano!". But so far as the world's most expensive, high-quality grapes like Chardonnay and Cabernet Sauvignon are concerned, they have powerful personalities that make wines made from them easily identifiable.

Varietal labelling

It was this ease of recognition that led the Californians (never a slouch at marketing) during the 1970s to name and label their wines after the grape variety they were made from. This move has probably had more impact on the wine drinking world than any other in recent years. Varietals – the name given to wines made from a single grape variety – have given wine drinkers great confidence. Not only is it now easier to predict what a wine will taste like, but we can now remember and pronounce its name without making fools of ourselves. Now even the French are putting the name of the grape on such traditional wines as burgundy.

This emphasis on grape varieties has also had an effect on quality. The traditional way of making wine – still practised in Bordeaux and many other parts of Europe – used to be to blend several grape varieties together. If you had problems with the weather when you were harvesting one grape, you could always up the percentage of another. Now that winemakers don't have that option to fall back on, they have to ensure that the basic quality of their grapes is as high as possible and that they're handled as carefully as possible in the winery.

So why then does a wine from the same grape variety sometimes taste so different? There are many factors at play and the most important is climate. Generally, vines grown in hot, sunny climates will have richer, riper fruit flavours than ones grown in cool, unpredictable ones. And, particularly in the northern hemisphere, weather conditions at harvest time can vary significantly from one year to another. A good vintage will result in a more full-bodied style: a poor vintage in a lighter, tarter one.

Other factors that play a part are the clones (the specific strain of a grape variety) that are planted, how old the vines are (older vines tend to make more expressive wines than younger ones) and how prolifically they're allowed to grow. If you allow vines to produce as many grapes as they can, you'll end up with a lighter, more dilute wine than if you restrict the yield or select only the best bunches.

Grapes, soils and ageing

Some grapes are ideally suited to certain sites – an affinity that the French enshrine in their strict *appellation contrôlée* system. Pinot Noir, for example, is perfectly suited to the relatively cool climate and limestone soils of Burgundy. (In fact a grape like Cabernet Franc would probably happily grow there too, but the French believe, with some justification, that it blurs the distinctiveness of the wines produced by different regions to allow winemakers to plant any grape they want.)

The character of a grape can also be modified or enhanced in the winery, most notably by the presence or absence of oak, and whether or not it is blended with other grape varieties. A Chardonnay that is made in a stainless steel tank and released within a few months of harvesting will be lighter and crisper than one which is aged in a barrel for several months. It will also be less obviously Chardonnay-like if it is blended with another strongly flavoured grape like Sémillon or Sauvignon, or even with a small proportion of an aromatic grape like Viognier. (In many wine producing regions producers can include up to 20 per cent of other grapes in a blend without having to state it on the label.)

The final important factor that can affect the way a grape tastes is age. Most wines nowadays are sold within months of being bottled and consumed within days of being bought. But if you buy an older wine, or keep it for a long time before you drink it, you will notice a marked change from the lively fruity character it had when it was young, a change you may or may not welcome.

All this means that although the chances are that if you like one wine made from a specific grape variety, you'll like others, that won't invariably be the case. Young, unoaked Tempranillo is as different from mature Rioja as Australian Chardonnay is from Chablis. Although most people have embraced the upfront fruity flavours of New World wines, others find them far too sweet and hanker for drier, more traditional versions.

The key is to know more about the styles of wine that are made with different grapes. Here are the ones you're most likely to come across.

Above *These cool European vineyards (Médoc), even if planted with the same grape variety as hot New World vineyards such as here in California (**far left**) will produce wines with quite different flavours. The cooler the climate, the leaner the flavours and conversely, in hotter climates, the wines have distinctly more tropical fruit flavours.*

THE MOST INFLUENTIAL WHITE GRAPES

Chardonnay

This grape variety is so overwhelmingly popular these days that it has almost become like a brand name. Most people associate it with the big, upfront, fruity flavours of Australia without realising that it is the grape that produces such well-known white burgundies as Chablis and that it is an important component of champagne.

Why is Chardonnay so popular? Because it is a grape variety that pleases everybody: the winemaker because it is easy to grow and will accommodate itself to whatever he or she wants to do with it. The wine drinker because it offers such a wide range of taste sensations from crisp, fresh and citrussy to powerfully full-bodied and oaky. The common denominator of all Chardonnay wines, however, is that they tend to be smooth and creamy (as opposed to crisply acidic like a Riesling or Sauvignon).

The major differences in style reflect the climate in which it is grown. Chardonnay which is grown in a cool region such as Chablis and the rest of Burgundy is leaner, drier and crisper than Chardonnay grown in warmer regions such as Australia, New Zealand, South Africa and the Languedoc, which has much riper, more tropical fruit flavours. It can acquire a slightly citrussy character, as it tends to in Chile or in the Limoux region of southern France. And it will be markedly different depending on whether or not it is oaked. Unoaked Chardonnay has crisp, clean fruit flavours (drier in Burgundy, riper in the southern hemisphere), while oaked Chardonnay ranges from the elegant creamy, nutty wines of Burgundy and California, to the more toasty oaky flavours of the less expensive Chardonnays of Eastern Europe, Spain and South Africa.

Chardonnay is frequently blended with either a complementary grape such as Sémillon and, to a lesser extent, Sauvignon (*see* below) or with less distinguished varieties such as Chenin, Colombard or Viura which are introduced to keep down the overall cost of the wine.

Sauvignon Blanc

An extraordinary range of styles are embraced by this variety, though most people associate it with the crisp, tart, green gooseberry flavour that is typical of New Zealand and to a lesser extent Loire Sauvignons. Like Chardonnay, it reveals different personalities depending on where it is planted, but its most appealing character and characteristic crisp acidity develops really only in cooler growing areas.

It also responds less well than Chardonnay to oak which tends to mask rather than enhance its natural crisp acidity. In top Sauvignons oak can give the wine added richness and longevity. But in younger wines, such as California's Fumé Blanc style, it creates a different, much softer style of wine that won't necessarily appeal if you are a Sauvignon aficionado. For most producers there is little point in oaking as inexpensive Sauvignon is best consumed young.

The great heartland of Sauvignon production is the Loire Valley which produces a distinctively crisp, minerally, flinty style, most commonly encountered in Sancerre and Pouilly-Fumé and in such lesser known appellations as Quincy and Menetou-Salon. In Bordeaux it achieves greatness in combination with Sémillon (see below) though it also makes pleasant, fresh, citrussy wines on its own account. Elsewhere in Europe the best bargains are to be found in Hungary whose winemakers manage to reproduce to a remarkable extent those grassy, gooseberryish flavours you find in the top wines.

In the southern hemisphere, New Zealand's Marlborough region has become the benchmark for New World Sauvignon, delivering a piercing intensity of fruit that, so far, remains unmatched anywhere else in the world. But it is increasingly being challenged by Chile and South Africa, both of which have producers who make some fine, elegant wines, as well as a large number of simple, straightforward, citrussy Sauvignons that offer excellent value to wine drinkers.

Riesling

Although it is capable of producing some of the world's finest and most individual wines, Riesling can be difficult to get used to. In its youth it can be sharply acidic and can take several years to develop those luscious oily, petrolly flavours that so please its devotees. But there is no other grape quite like it. Infinitely refreshing, elegant and juicy, it's like biting into a perfectly ripe grape.

Germany is indisputably the home of great Riesling, though it varies from region to region, from the thrillingly racy acidity of the Mosel to more opulent, rich, spicy flavours of the Pfalz and Rheingau, and in levels of sweetness from fresh, crisp, appley Kabinetts to sumptuously sweet Beerenauslesen and Trockenbeerenauslesen. Serious Rieslings are also produced in Alsace, where they tend to be richer and more alcoholic than the German examples, and in the Wachau region of Austria.

Above *Sauvignon Blanc is a highly adaptable grape variety. Classic examples are from the upper reaches of the Loire Valley in France and are lean, crisp and grassy. More pungent, intensely flavoured examples come from New Zealand.*

Far left *Chardonnay is not simply the name of a wine. It is a grape variety producing wines that range from crisp, minerally wines from Chablis, Mâcon and northern Italy, right through to the rich, tropical, oaky blockbusters from California and Australia.*

Riesling has also found a natural home in the New World – in the cooler growing areas of South Australia (especially the Clare Valley), where it develops a richer, limier, and for first-time Riesling drinkers, a more attractively fruity character. The grape also does well in New Zealand, Canada and New York State.

Sémillon

A grape that is less appreciated than it deserves as it is often blended. On its own it makes richly textured wines with wonderful flavours of caramelised pineapple and tropical fruits. That pineapple flavour still comes through when it is combined with other grapes (most commonly Sauvignon Blanc and Chardonnay) but Sémillon rarely gets the credit.

In the Hunter Valley in New South Wales it produces extraordinarily luscious wines that last for years. But it is the real star of white wine making in Bordeaux where, with Sauvignon, it produces fine dry whites along with the famous sweet wine, Sauternes.

Chenin Blanc

Easy to grow, generously productive, Chenin Blanc has become a popular choice among New World winemakers, especially in South Africa. Although capable of producing attractive, smoothly rounded whites, it can be searingly sharp or unpleasantly vegetal. However, in the right hands its crisp, clean flavours can be reminiscent of a light Chardonnay.

It is almost a different grape altogether in the Loire Valley in France where it is used to make a unique range of dry, off-dry and sweet wines with incredibly honeyed flavours that develop with age. It is also the basis of sparkling wines like Saumur and Crémant de Loire.

Important but lesser-known white grape varieties

Colombard A high yielding grape variety that in France serves the dual role of providing the base for Cognac and Armagnac and of producing crisp, uncomplicated, slightly floral white wines, most notably Vin de Pays des Côtes de Gascogne.

Colombard is also planted in the New World – in California, South Africa and Australia – where it develops a riper, more tropical fruit flavour and can be used as an inexpensive substitute for or blended with Chardonnay.

Gewürztraminer A love-it-or-loathe-it grape variety with a highly distinctive, pungent, aromatic character whose taste has been compared to lychees, rose petals and Turkish delight. Its finest expression is in Alsace in France where it is used to make remarkable luscious, long-lived, semi-sweet and dessert wines.

There is also increasing interest in Gewürztraminer (or Gewürz, as it is known for short) in the New World. South Africa, Chile and Oregon all offer attractively fruity examples.

Muscat Of all grape varieties this is the one that tastes the most truly grapey. Although you may come across it in dry wines, labelled as Dry Muscat or in blends, its reputation is built on dessert wines. It presents itself in an extraordinary number of guises, from the soft, gently sparkling Moscato d'Asti, to the light, honeyed, refreshing Moscatel de Valencia, to the rich, sweet, fortified Muscats of southern France like Muscat de Beaumes de Venise. Muscat is also grown in the Rutherglen region of Victoria in Australia where it produces a richly toffeed liqueur wine.

Pinot Gris/Pinot Grigio The two different names this grape goes by reflect two very different styles. Pinot Grigio, as it is known in Italy, produces a typically crisp, clean white wine that should be drunk as young as possible. Pinot Gris, which is a speciality of the Alsace region of France, is richer and more opulent, producing wines that range in style from dry and full-bodied to luxuriously sweet and which have an impressive capacity for ageing. There has also been a fair amount of New World interest in it, particularly in Oregon, as a stylish alternative to Chardonnay.

Viognier A few years ago almost no-one had heard of this exotically perfumed grape, which is the mainstay of the equally obscure but expensive northern Rhône wine, Condrieu. Since then, there have been extensive plantings in the Languedoc and in the New World, particularly California. Like Muscat, a small amount of Viognier in a blend will have a disproportionate impact and can easily be identified by its aromatic, slightly apricotty aroma.

Above *Gewürztraminer, with its delicately pink grapes is something you either love or hate. The wine it produces has distinctively exotic aromas (and is often the perfect foil for Chinese and Southeast Asian cuisine).*

Far left *Riesling is a grape variety that produces some of the world's most exciting wines. Its refreshing acidity gives the wines great elegance and as they range from crisp and appley to lusciously sweet and honeyed, they partner a wide variety of food.*

THE MOST INFLUENTIAL RED GRAPES

Cabernet Sauvignon

This grape is to red wine what Chardonnay is to white – almost every winemaker wants to plant it and every wine lover to drink it.

It is distinguished by its small, thick-skinned grapes, which give structure and body, making it suitable for long ageing. Seldom light-bodied, Cabernet wines can be very different, depending on whether they come from the comparatively northern region of Bordeaux, where the variety produces dry, elegant, occasionally austere wines, or from the much hotter southern hemisphere, where a vibrant blackcurrant character is more evident.

Even within Bordeaux there is a world of difference between the simple fruit of a young claret and the velvety opulence of a 10-year-old classed growth from a great vintage. Traditionally, Cabernet-dominated wines come from the so-called "left bank" of the Gironde, from famous Médoc villages such as St-Estèphe, St-Julien, Pauillac and Margaux. Even though they are blended with a proportion of Merlot, they are characteristically leaner and less fruity than those from the Merlot-dominated "right bank".

An altogether fruitier style is produced in the New World, particularly in the Coonawarra region of South Australia, where the wines acquire an intensely lush, minty character. Chile produces wines that have a particularly vivid fruit flavour, while South Africa's tend to be leaner and more European in character. The wine growing region that models its Cabernets most closely on the classic French style is California, whose wines rival Bordeaux in both quality and price.

Merlot

The reputation of this grape variety has never really risen to the dizzy heights of Cabernet Sauvignon despite the fact that it is more widely planted in Bordeaux and is the backbone of one of the world's most sought after wines, Château Pétrus. Regarded by the Bordelais primarily as a useful blending partner to Cabernet, it has benefited enormously from New World interest because its supple fruit makes it a more approachable starting point for the growing number of new red wine drinkers.

Merlot's character also doesn't vary as much as Cabernet. Even without oak it generally makes a soft fruity red, though more expensive versions will develop a particularly velvety texture or rich, lush chocolatey tones.

Unlike Cabernet Sauvignon, Merlot seldom suffers from being under ripe and drinks as enjoyably young and fruity as it does with a year or two of bottle age.

In the New World the most exciting Merlots are to be found in Chile and up on the west coast of America in California and Washington State. South African Merlot can be robustly plummy, while in New Zealand, it is being blended with their slightly lean Cabernet to very good effect.

Pinot Noir

They say you're either a Cabernet or a burgundy fan but for Pinot Noir devotees there's simply no contest. Other grapes may come in and out of fashion but there is no grape that matches it for sheer sensuality.

Fine Pinot Noir is an elusive goal. Good burgundy is as much about feel as flavour and not many areas can achieve that thrillingly fine, silky, texture or pure, heady raspberry fruit – a flavour that fades to a rich, truffley gaminess with age. Elsewhere in France, Alsace and the Loire can provide pale, though perfectly pleasant, imitations, while in the New World impressively Burgundian-style Pinots are produced in Oregon, the cooler parts of California and in New Zealand.

In hotter climates Pinot Noir tends to develop a more deeply fruity, character quite different from the Burgundian one. Romania, for example, produces some full-bodied versions, as do Spain and Italy. Pinot Noir is also successfully grown in Austria (where it is known as Blauburgunder), Germany (where it is called Spätburgunder) and Switzerland. Of the remaining New World wine areas, Australia's cooler Yarra Valley has found success with Pinot Noir, as has South Africa and Chile which, like its other reds, produces Pinot with vivid fruit flavours.

Syrah/Shiraz

Many people don't realise that these are one and the same grape. It produces gutsy wines with a characteristic smoky, slightly tarry aroma, vivid red berry fruit and a distinctive spicy peppery finish.

The finest examples come from the northern Rhône, producing massively concentrated, big wines, such as Hermitage and Cornas. Syrah is also widely planted in the southern Rhône, where it tends to be blended with Grenache which gives the resulting wine a softer, suppler character. It gives backbone, too, to many southern French reds.

Above Merlot has a softer, more approachable style than Cabernet Sauvignon and in the clay soils of St-Emilion and Pomerol, on Bordeaux's right bank, it produces two of the world's most expensive and illustrious wines – Châteaux Pétrus and Le Pin.

Far left Cabernet Sauvignon has small berries, thick skins, high levels of pips and is ideally suited to extended oak ageing. Cabernet makes wines that, at their finest, can age for decades and the majority of these come from Bordeaux's Médoc district.

But the country that has done more than any other to put Shiraz (as they call it) on the map is Australia. Much sweeter and fruitier than French Syrah, it has the same impressive concentration. There is also Syrah in Argentina, some in California and an increasing amount in South Africa (where they also call it Shiraz).

Important but lesser-known red grape varieties

Cabernet Franc Even more than Merlot, Cabernet Franc is the unsung hero of Bordeaux, a valuable component of many blends thanks to its ability to ripen earlier and tolerate cool weather better than Cabernet Sauvignon. It is lighter, fruitier and more acidic than the other Cabernet, though in the New World (such California, South Africa and New York and Washington States), it is capable of producing wines of great power and personality.

Cabernet Franc is also widely found in southwest France, in Eastern Europe and in the Friuli region of Italy. But the area where it really shines is in the central part of the Loire Valley where it produces charmingly elegant, fruity reds such as Bourgueil, Chinon and Saumur-Champigny.

Gamay Most people have heard of Beaujolais. Few realise that Gamay is the grape from which it is made. It has a distinctive character – light, juicy and fruity with, when it is made in a *nouveau* style, an inimitable bubble-gum-and-banana flavour and aroma. It is also found in the Loire where it is used to make Beaujolais-style reds.

Grenache/Garnacha The world's most widely planted red wine grape – a silent partner in many of the Rhône's best known reds (from Côtes du Rhône to Châteauneuf-du-Pâpe), in the wines of the Languedoc and Roussillon and in Spain. Generously prolific, Grenache has traditionally been used for rather light, dilute strawberry flavoured reds, but renewed interest in it, and particularly in the wines that can be produced from older vines, has resulted in lusher, more full-bodied examples. Some fine New World Grenache wines are emerging from Australia and California, where along with other Rhône varieties the variety has been enthusiastically embraced.

Mourvèdre A richly perfumed, yet powerful grape variety that features in many southern French reds, especially in Provence where it is the dominant variety in Bandol. It is also widely planted in southern

Spain where it is called Monastrell and produces powerful, full-bodied gamey reds such as Jumilla. In Australia it is called Mataro and often blended with Shiraz.

Nebbiolo This grape variety is the backbone of two of northwest Italy's greatest reds, Barolo and Barbaresco. A deeply flavoured, dense, late-ripening variety, it has unyielding tannins that can take several years of wood maturation to smooth out. But the results can be magnificent.

Pinotage A cross between Pinot Noir and Cinsault (or Hermitage as it used to be called by the South Africans), Pinotage is South Africa's great glory – though its character depends critically on how it's made. If the vines are allowed to crop prolifically it produces simple gluggable, sweetish reds. If yields are kept low and the grapes come from old vines, it can produce deliciously deep, rich concentrated full-bodied wines.

Sangiovese Until recently the name Sangiovese was rarely seen on a wine bottle, although it is widely used in Italy for the production of Chianti and many other Italian reds. It most commonly results in light, fruity, supple wines with relatively high levels of acidity, though, in some denominations like Brunello di Montalcino, and as a component of so-called Super-Tuscans, it can make very serious wine indeed.

Tempranillo Spain's most highly regarded grape goes by a confusing variety of names – Tempranillo in Rioja (of which it is a major component), Tinto Fino in Ribera del Duero and Cencibel in Valdepeñas. Young, unoaked Tempranillo is vividly fruity, but that character has often been subdued by extended oak contact, particularly in wines labelled "Reserva" or "Gran Reserva" which have several years in cask and bottle before they are released. The resulting wines have a distinctive soft strawberry fruit.

Zinfandel California's great grape which like Pinotage makes an extraordinary range of wines from sweet blush coloured "white" Zinfandel to richly alcoholic "killer Zins" of 14 degrees (the more interesting wines by far). It is not planted as such within Europe (though southern Italy's Primitivo is believed to be the same grape). There have also been some successful examples from South Africa.

Above *Syrah (Shiraz) produces some of the world's most powerful wines. The benchmark examples come from the northern Rhône in France and from the Barossa and Hunter Valleys in Australia. They have the common characteristic of being dark coloured and tannic with intense fruit and peppery spice.*

Far left *Pinot Noir, in contrast, produces some of the most delicate and subtle red wines. It is notoriously difficult to handle, being susceptible to mould, but can produce exquisitely ethereal, sensuous wines and consequently has legions of loyal followers.*

CLIMATE, SOIL AND VINES

If there's one thing Old and New World winemakers agree about it is the need for top quality grapes. With them the least talented winemaker can make decent wine. Without them even the best will struggle.

But how do you produce them? In Europe, especially France, traditionally, the best way to ensure quality is to find a vineyard with the ideal soil, position and climate for the grapes you want to grow – what the the French call *terroir*. This is enshrined in the closely monitored set of rules and regulations of the *appellation contrôlée* system which determines which grape varieties can be used, how densely they can be planted and how many grapes (how great a yield) they can produce.

For newer wine producing countries, the emphasis up to now has been more on the management of the vineyard – how to prune and train the vines to best ripen the fruit. There are no hang-ups about irrigation or about machine pruning or harvesting – everything is done to maximise the efficiency of the vines.

As with other aspects of winemaking, the divisions between the two approaches are less clear cut than they once were. French winemakers now pay more attention to training and pruning. Australian wine producers are more aware of the advantages of planting the right grapes on the right site. More important than either tradition these days is the type of wine being made – whether it is an inexpensive wine for immediate consumption or a fine wine that will command a high price and therefore justifies extra attention in the vineyard.

But even the most meticulous planning and control cannot wholly determine how a wine turns out. Grapes are a natural harvest like any other and in the end they depend on something that is fundamentally unpredictable – the weather.

The importance of climate

Vines are hardy plants but they will not grow just anywhere. Too cold and the grapes won't ripen. Too hot and they won't develop the fresh fruity flavours you're looking for. To cultivate vines successfully you need a sufficiently cold winter so that the plants can go into hibernation and regain their vigour, which is why people don't make wine on the equator.

As important as temperature is sunlight which creates the process of photosynthesis that develops sugar in grapes. The reason why grapes ripen successfully in comparatively cool areas like Germany is that they have long sunny days at harvest time. Grapes will struggle to ripen even in a comparatively warm region if there isn't enough sun.

Rainfall/humidity Vines can't live without water but they can survive in a surprisingly dry climate. In fact, the more stressed they are and the more they dig down their roots to absorb nutrients from the soil, the better quality grapes they tend to produce. What winemakers ideally want is rain at the right time – during the winter and spring rather than in the middle of the harvest when it can damage the crop. Some degree of humidity is useful, particularly for the development of botrytis (the sought-after type of rot that afflicts grapes destined for dessert wines), but too much can lead to disease and less healthy types of rot.

Moderate climates Continental climates with hot summers and harsh winters can be harder to handle than more moderate maritime-influenced ones. In Washington State in northwestern America, for example, vines are damaged by the severe winter conditions about one year in six. In hot climates, on the other hand, some fluctuation between day and night temperatures is valuable, particularly for white wines – preserving freshness and adequate levels of acidity. Winemakers also ideally want to avoid an area that is regularly hit by strong winds or which is particularly susceptible to frost.

Vintage variations Regardless of the overall climate, weather conditions vary from one year to the next. This matters not just at harvest time, but in spring when the vines are budding and flowering. If the weather is unusually cold or wet, then not enough flowers will be fertilised and the number of bunches of grapes will be reduced.

Most weather conditions are outside the wine producer's control, though surprisingly they can, given access to the right equipment, mitigate the effect of frost by the use of heaters, helicopters or wind machines which can agitate the air and prevent the temperature from falling below freezing. Sprinklers can also be used which protect the young shoots by covering them with a layer of ice. Heavy rain and hail are potentially far more serious, particularly near harvest time, as they can split the grapes and cause them to rot.

There tends to be less vintage variation in the New World than in regions which are at the margin of grape-growing viability, including classic European regions such as the Loire, Burgundy and Germany. The effect is less disastrous in areas where the produce of one vintage is blended with those of previous years as in Champagne.

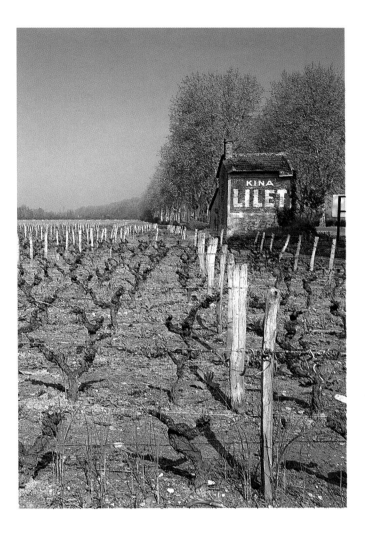

Above *Gravelly soil around Bordeaux reveals how superficially poor looking soil is often ideal for wine production forcing the vine to dig deep for moisture and nutrients.*

Far left *These neatly tended, widely spaced rows in California epitomise modern, large-scale, commercial vineyard practice. They have been specially laid out to facilitate as much mechanisation as possible (both pruning and harvesting are often now done by machine).*

Choosing the best site

The ideal site for one style of wine may not necessarily be the best for another. If you intend to make a light, inexpensive, fruity wine for early consumption, you want a site that's easily managed, giving the largest possible crop. If your ambitions are for a more serious wine, you'll look for a vineyard that produces fewer grapes, but much better quality ones.

Aspect In spite of the overall climate of a region, it is possible to find a particularly favourable microclimate – a range of hills that catches the rainfall so that it is usually dry the other side or, as in coastal areas like California, cooling fogs or morning mists that roll in off the sea. Also important is the direction the vineyard faces. In cooler areas you want slopes that attract the maximum amount of sun.

Which type of vineyard you have access to affects the kind of wine you can make. For example, if you want to make a light, citrussy style of Chardonnay, you'll need grapes that are produced on a cooler site and probably at a higher altitude than the richer, more tropical fruit flavours you'd get from grapes grown on the warmer valley floor.

Soil Unlike other crops, the winemaker is not looking for highly fertile soil as this can result in overproductive vines that produce far too many leaves and not enough grapes. The ideal soil is well-drained without getting waterlogged, but which stores moisture within reach of the vine's deep-reaching roots. Some of the best vineyards look surprisingly inhospitable, scattered with flat stones, in which it seems surprising that any plant can grow. These stones, though, can assist the ripening process by absorbing heat during the day, then reflecting it back on the vine at night.

There are certain distinctive soils which give the wine a particular flavour and character (referred to by the French as *goût de terroir*). Among them is the mineral-rich "terra rossa" soil of Coonawarra in South Australia which lends a particularly intense quality to the Cabernet Sauvignon grown there, as is the ancient limestone and clay soil of Chablis which helps to give the wine its steely, minerally quality.

Planting the right grapes

Having selected the vineyard the producer has to decide which type of grapes to grow in it. There is, for example, no point in planting a grape like Shiraz (Syrah) – that needs a hot climate to ripen properly – in

Germany, or one that needs a long, slow ripening period – like Riesling – in California's Central Valley. Some grapes like Pinot Noir and Mourvèdre are notoriously difficult to handle and so would not be a viable choice if you could not expect to get a decent return for your wines.

Clones Within the grape variety selected, the producer then chooses which clones or strains to plant. This decision is based on a variety of considerations, some commercial, some stylistic. Some clones are higher yielding than others and have greater resistance to disease. Others may be more typical of a style of wine that the producer wants to emulate, for instance, white or red burgundy. Often he only learns by trial and error which clones work best in his vineyards; many producers in Oregon, for example, found that a Burgundian clone of Chardonnay was better suited to their comparatively cool climate than clones first imported from California, a much warmer wine region. For that reason, many winemakers hedge their bets and plant several different clones.

Rootstocks Since the re-appearance of phylloxera, the deadly disease that wiped out much of world's vineyards in the last century, many vines are now grafted onto a separate set of roots or rootstock that is resistant to the pest. Apart from giving immunity to the disease, the selection of a particular kind of rootstock is another tool that can be used to control or encourage the vine's vigour.

Density How close or far apart you plant your vines can also determine how productive they are, though, in the New World the decision is more likely to rest on whether they are sufficiently spaced to allow a mechanical harvester to pass through. In fertile conditions planting closely means that vines at least have to compete for the abundant nutrients available to them. In an arid, dry area you may want to give the plants a better chance of survival by planting them further apart.

Age of vines The style of a wine can also be affected by the age of the vines. Younger vines (those established for at least three years) tend to have an attractive fruitiness, but little depth or complexity. Older vines of 20 to 30 years are generally less productive, but create wines that are more intense. Most commercial wines come from grapes that are somewhere in between. Winemakers who use older vines usually highlight the fact on the label using the terms "Old Vine" or "Vieilles Vignes".

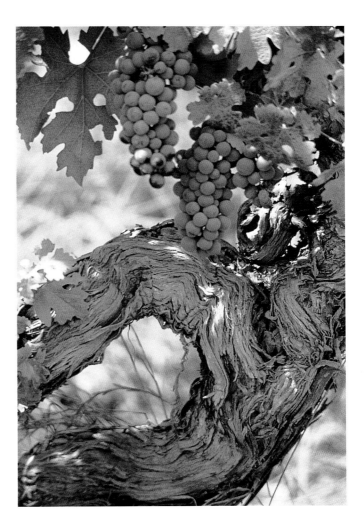

Above *This 100-year-old Shiraz vine, with its spectacularly gnarled trunk, is still very much in business as can be seen here. It may not produce many bunches, but the grapes should produce a wine with good concentration and complexity.*

Far left *These large, pale stones in the soil of this vineyard in Châteauneuf-du-Pape are known as pudding stones. They are vital to the ripening of the grapes as they retain the warmth from the sun and reflect it back up to the vines.*

Managing the vines

Left to themselves vines grow prolifically – a good thing, you might have thought – but what the wine producer wants is good quality grapes, not luxuriant vegetation. There are several ways of achieving this.

Training and trellising If you've travelled through a wine region, you will have seen the difference between the traditional "bush vine" and the typical modern vineyard with neat rows of elegantly trained vines. Good wine can be made from both, but for practical reasons winemakers prefer the more modern system of trellising, allowing them to prune and harvest mechanically. It also allows them to reposition vine shoots to ensure the grapes get maximum exposure to the sun.

Pruning How drastically a vine should be pruned is open to argument, but most producers carry out some form of winter pruning to control the number of shoots, and consequently bunches of grapes, produced by the vine the following year. A summer pruning (*vendange verte*) can be carried out to further restrict the number of bunches or size of the yield.

More emphasis is now put on controlling the amount of leaves or 'canopy' the vine produces. If it is too prolific all the energy goes into the leaves rather than the fruit. By removing leaves or taking out shoots, a producer can markedly affect the resulting grapes. With Sauvignon, for example, he can either accentuate the grassy, gooseberry character of the grapes by leaving them in the shade, or cut the leaves right back and expose the grapes to the sun for riper, more tropical flavours.

Irrigating This is an emotive subject in Europe and even forbidden in some areas. The argument is that too much watering dilutes the juice – but most European vineyards enjoy a perfectly adequate level of rainfall. In some New World wine regions vines would die without irrigation and there need be no loss of quality with sophisticated modern drip irrigation systems that deliver precisely measured amounts of water to the vine.

Treatment/spraying Eradicating pests and diseases doesn't actually affect the style of the wine other than providing good raw materials to work on in the form of healthy grapes. The general trend is towards a more natural "green" approach, keeping the use of chemicals and fertilisers to a minimum and encouraging natural "cover crops" and insect populations to check disease and over-rapid growth instead.

Harvesting the grapes

Choosing the right moment to harvest is one of the most crucial decisions the wine producer takes and the easiest to get wrong. If he picks before the grapes are fully ripe, the wine may suffer from sharp, acidic or green, sappy flavours. If he leaves them on the vine too long they may lose their freshness and go flabby. And there's always the risk of a sudden storm blowing up which will spoil the crop entirely. Modern winemakers assess the state of their vineyards constantly, checking the ripeness of the grapes daily by appearance, taste and chemical analysis.

Although the ideal harvesting time depends on the type of wine being made (for champagne and sparkling wine it is better to pick grapes while they still have a high level of acidity), these days, producers are inclined to accept a higher level of risk and leave the grapes to ripen for as long as possible. A winemaker may in fact make a feature of this as in "Late Picked" or "Late Harvest" dessert wines.

Machine or hand picking Although theoretically this is a choice, in reality, the decision to machine or hand pick depends on practical considerations. The main ones are whether the vineyards are designed for machine harvesting, whether there is a suitable pool of skilled labour to pick the grapes and whether the regulations governing the region permit machine harvesting (in Champagne, for example, they don't).

Machine harvesting has the advantage of being quick, reliable and relatively cheap – and harvesting can take place at night when the grapes are at their coolest. Hand harvesting, on the other hand, can be more precise and is vital where some kind of selection is required, for example, when picking grapes in a vineyard affected by botrytis. Most traditional estates in regions such as Bordeaux, Burgundy and the Mosel still pick by hand, as do countries with a cheap labour force like South Africa and Chile. Australian grapes are mostly machine picked.

Keeping the grapes cool Next to deciding the right moment to pick, this is the most important aspect of harvesting. The danger of picking grapes in the heat of the day is that they will start to oxidise and lose their freshness, so most harvesting – whether by hand or machine – takes place in the early morning, if not at night. If there is a significant distance for the grapes to travel, they may well be transported to the winery in refrigerated trucks, or even crushed in a temperature-controlled crushing station nearer the vineyard.

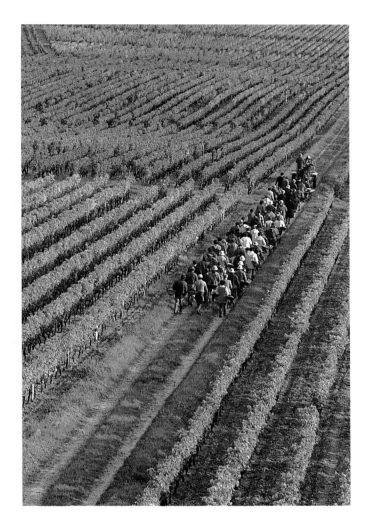

Above *Pickers at Château d'Yquem, Sauternes. Pickers may have to go through the vineyards as many a half a dozen times, each time selecting the grapes most affected by botrytis. This is the key to making fine late harvest wines and is time consuming, risky and hugely expensive.*

Far left *These hoses running along the vines are for drip irrigation, illegal in most parts of Europe, but widely used in the hotter, drier parts of the New World. They can be computer controlled to give each vine precisely the right "dose" of water.*

WINEMAKING

If you walked into a large, modern winery you would be amazed; huge stainless steel tanks run from floor to ceiling, encased in a network of ladders, hoses and pumps. Banks of computerised controls monitor the temperature of each tank minute by minute. Fork-lift trucks bustle noisily around, moving barrels around cellars the size of a football pitch. It is a far cry from the romantic image of the small, French wine producer with a couple of concrete tanks and a few barrels in a cobweb-festooned outhouse (though they still exist). And yet, fundamentally, wine is made in the same way from crushed grapes that are fermented into alcohol.

The big difference is in the amount of control that winemakers now have. For many small winemakers it used to be something of a hit and miss affair, but now, within the limits of the fruit they have available, winemakers can more or less do what they want. They can control the fermentation temperature so that even in the hottest vine growing areas you can make fresh fruity wine. They don't have to use expensive barrels to get oaky flavours, they can use chips. They have access to sophisticated machines like ultra-gentle presses and filters which preserve rather than strip out flavour, and a battery of laboratory equipment to measure what they are doing at every stage.

How much of this bag of tricks a winemaker will employ depends on what part of the world he is operating in, how well-equipped his winery is and how expensive a wine is being made. In some areas certain techniques are not permitted (for example the use of oak chips). With cheaper wines the aim is to produce a simple, fresh fruity wine and bottle it as quickly as possible. With finer wines the emphasis is more on being able to treat different batches of grapes different ways. To what extent a winemaker can do this depends on the relatively mundane matter of how many tanks and barrels he has to play around with.

Like any other craftsmen, winemakers have their own ways of doing things. Some take more risks, allowing their wines to ferment at higher than average temperatures, use wild yeasts and refuse to filter. Others are more inclined to play safe. But broadly the options are as follows.

Making white wine

The biggest and most obvious difference between white and red wine-making is colour. With white wines you don't want the juice to pick up colour from the skins – the grapes are pressed and the juice run off before fermentation rather than afterwards as with red wines. The winemaker's main objective is to preserve the grapes' natural fresh aromas and flavours – keeping the juice cool and protecting it from air. This is done partly physically by keeping it in a covered container and partly through the addition of sulphur and ascorbic acid which mop up the excess oxygen that can brown the grapes and dull their flavour.

The first step is to crush the grapes to release the juice. This is done as gently as possible so as not to split the pips which contain harsh woody flavours. For the same reason the stems are normally removed. This releases a certain amount of juice called the free-run juice which has a particularly pure fruit flavour and so may well be handled separately.

If the winemaker wants to extract extra body and flavour from the skins, he may leave the must (the mass of juice and skins) to soak for a couple of hours in the press or in a refrigerated tank for a few hours before he presses it. Again the press is likely to be designed to be as gentle as possible to avoid squeezing out harsh stalky flavours. The juice is then clarified either by filtering or settling (lowering the temperature so that the solids fall to the bottom of the tank), then pumped off into a holding tank or a fermentation tank. The object is to start the fermentation with the cleanest, freshest possible juice.

Which yeast? In order to get the fermentation started the winemaker needs to add yeast. In the past, wild yeasts that existed in the winery and on the skins of the grapes themselves were used, but these days most winemakers work with cultured yeasts (i.e. those grown in a laboratory). The advantage is not only that they are much more reliable and won't stop working halfway through, but that they can also accentuate certain fruity and floral aromas and flavours in the grapes.

Whether to chaptalise The addition of sugar (chaptalisation) is done to boost the alcohol content of the grapes. It is routine in some regions such as northern Europe, but not permitted in others such as Australia.

Fermentation techniques In general, the fermentation temperatures are at about 12–15°C for simple, fresh, fruity whites and higher for fuller-bodied whites (18–20°C), allowing the development of more complex flavours. The juice may be simply fermented in stainless steel to retain its freshness. For fuller-bodied styles, it may be fermented with oak chips or staves, or it could be barrel fermented – a technique that gives a particularly rich, creamy character. Alternatively, a combination of techniques will be used and the resulting wines blended together.

*These are not perhaps the images you would expect of producers in Bordeaux (**above**) and Châteauneuf-du-Pape (**far left**), but they illustrate how much winemaking has moved away from the romantic images of barrels in dusty cellars. These small producers may still be in existence, but they are eclipsed by modern, well-equipped wineries which have greater control over their winemaking.*

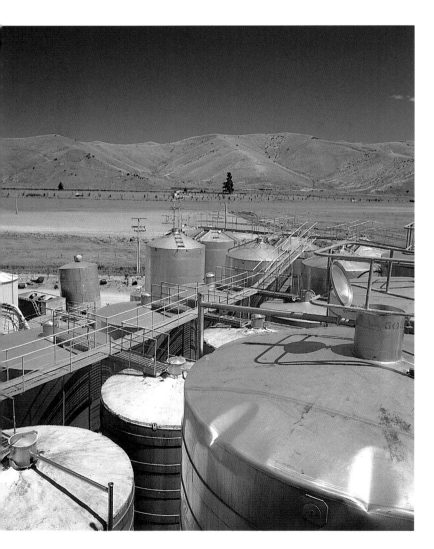

In the case of dry whites, the fermentation would be allowed to continue until all the sugar in the grapes had been converted to alcohol. If a slightly sweeter, medium-dry wine was required, the fermentation might be stopped before that point (usually by the addition of sulphur), while some sugar was still left in the grapes.

Malolactic fermentation This second fermentation, or "malo" as it is sometimes called, converts the harsher malic acids in the wine into softer lactic acids. It can either happen spontaneously or it is induced by the addition of bacteria. With most red wines it is allowed to take place, but with whites, it is more of a conscious decision, depending on whether the winemaker wants to preserve a fresh, crisp edge to his wine or give it a richer, rounded, more buttery character.

Lees contact This is another way of enriching the flavour and texture of a wine. It involves leaving the wine on the lees – the spent yeast that has been used for fermentation – for several weeks, they may also be stirred from time to time. The technique is often carried out as part of the process of barrel fermentation, diminishing the oakier effects of new barrels.

Barrel maturation At least part of the blend (though not for fresh, crisp whites) may be either fermented in barrel or transferred to barrels after fermentation and aged for anything from a few weeks to several months (*see* pages 32–33). Apart from the obvious effect of giving the wine a more oaky, toasty flavour, wood differs from stainless steel in that it keeps the wine at a higher temperature and allows an amount of oxidation which leads to more complex flavours.

Fining and filtering With most fresh, fruity white wines, the wine would then simply be cleaned up before bottling. It would be chilled to precipitate tartrates (harmless but nonetheless slightly alarming-looking crystals that might otherwise appear in the bottle), then bentonite (a kind of clay) would be added to attract the larger particles remaining in the wine. These would then fall to the bottom of the tank and be discarded when the wine was pumped off (fining). Generally the wine will also be filtered, though winemakers now try to avoid excessive filtering as it strips out flavour. Further sulphur and ascorbic acid would be added to prevent the wine oxidising or re-fermenting in the bottle.

The winemaker might also adjust the acidity and sweetness of the wine at this stage. If it was too sharp, it could be chemically de-acidified. If it needed to be a little sweeter, he might add grape concentrate.

Blending options Much of the skill of the winemaker lies in using the components he has assembled to make a finished wine. Which ones he picks will depend on how many wines he intends to produce and at what kind of price. A large winery, for example, may produce several different wines for several different customers. A smaller estate may produce just two – a standard wine and a more expensive "reserve" wine. A typical mid-price New World Chardonnay, for example, will be a blend of about five or six components – 30 to 40 per cent aged in oak, a portion left unoaked and the remainder treated with different yeasts and with oak chips or staves. The winemaker will make up several different blends from these components to see which works best before he finally bottles and releases the wine.

Making red wine

The red-winemaker has different priorities from the white-winemaker. True, he wants fresh fruit flavour, but his primary concern is to get as much colour and flavour as possible from the skins of the grapes. And if he is seeking to make a wine that will last, he needs to get a base wine of sufficient intensity and concentration to support extended oak ageing.

In making a lighter red the main aim is to avoid excessive tannins so the grapes will be not only crushed but de-stemmed as well. Unlike white-winemaking, they then go straight into a fermentation tank – reds are fermented on their skins rather than from clear juice.

Carbonic maceration The exception to this procedure is a technique called carbonic maceration. Instead of being crushed, whole grapes are left in a tank under a layer of carbon dioxide and start to ferment spontaneously. The effect is to give bright fruit flavours and soft tannins. The technique is mainly used in Beaujolais but is also beneficial for grapes that can otherwise be very tough and tannic like Carignan.

Cold maceration This is another technique used for lighter reds. Basically, it involves soaking the crushed grapes in their own juice at a low temperature for anything from a week to three weeks and results in wine with a particularly fresh, fruity character.

Above Punching down the "cap" of grape skins with long poles during fermentation helps release flavour and colour from the skins. If a wine does not have enough structure and flavour, it will not support much ageing in oak – it will be overwhelmed by it.

Far left Stainless steel tanks with sophisticated temperature control are vital in hot regions. Traditionally, fermenting in warmer climates resulted in heavy, alcoholic wines with little fruit. Now that temperatures can be controlled, lively fruit flavours are retained.

Fermentation techniques Red wine fermentation starts in a similar way to that of whites. Yeast and possibly sugar or acid may be added (the former to boost the alcohol content, the latter to help preserve the colour and maintain a lively fruitiness). The grape must may also be warmed slightly to get the fermentation started and again, help to extract extra colour from the skins. The normal fermentation temperature for lighter reds is 22 to 26°C. For fuller-bodied wines temperatures may be allowed to rise to between 26 to 30°C and can even rise as high as 35°C.

As the fermentation takes off, the skins rise to the surface of the tank or container and have to be pushed back under the fermenting liquid otherwise they will dry out and won't yield up their colour or flavour. This can be done manually (or even by treading the grapes down) or mechanically. Alternatives are to keep the cap (the skins) permanently submerged, circulate the liquid in the tank and pump it over the skins, or drain off the wine from the bottom of the tank and return it to the top.

The aim with a light fruity red would be to complete this process as quickly as possible so the juice is not left in contact with the skins for more than a few days. In other cases, a proportion of the wine might be drawn off before the fermentation has completed and then put into barrels to finish its fermentation. This results in better integration of the oak and fruit.

For fuller-bodied wines, once the fermentation is complete, the winemaker might well leave a proportion of the fermented wine on the skins for a further period of three to four weeks before pressing to extract even more flavour and colour. Another way of concentrating the juice – which may be used in a poor vintage – is to run off a proportion of the juice after a limited amount of skin contact, which increases the ratio of skins to the remaining juice (this is basically the procedure that is used for making rosé).

Pressing the juice Once the fermentation is complete, the winemaker will run off the juice, then put the remaining mass of grapes and skins through a press. This richer, more robust "press wine" may be returned to the rest of the juice to give it extra body. For high quality wines, rather than crushing all the grapes, a proportion of the wine may be fermented from lightly crushed bunches or by treading the grapes by foot in the traditional way.

Adding oak Lighter red wines are unlikely to be barrel aged but, to make them fuller-flavoured, a New World winemaker may age part of the blend in a tank with oak chips.

As with white wines, red wines can be aged in a variety of different types of wood (*see* pages 32–33). An important part of this process is racking, a device by which the wine is deliberately exposed to air by moving it from one barrel to another. It is a way of making the wine mature more quickly and also of avoiding the unpleasant sulphury smells that can accumulate if wine is left in barrel for a long time. The winemaker may also opt to carry out the malolactic fermentation in barrel which again results in better integration of oak and fruit.

How long the wine spends in barrel – or maturing in the bottle – will depend very much on the price at which it is likely to be sold. Only producers of premium quality wines which are intended to last for several years (or those that are subject to regulations about the minimum age at which they can release their wines) are likely to age their wines for any length of time.

Fining and filtration Like white wines, light reds may be cold stabilised, and will simply be fined and filtered before bottling. A limited quantity of sulphur may also be added as a preservative.

Oak-ageing has a stabilising and preservative effect, so that wines that have spent time in barrel don't generally need as much fining and filtering as those that haven't. Whether you should filter at all in these circumstances is a matter of opinion. Some winemakers make a feature of the fact that their wines are unfiltered on the basis that filtering diminishes a wine's intensity. Others believe it is more important to have a stable, reliable product.

Tannin Any wine that is destined to last more than a couple of years needs a reasonable level of tannin – the preservative compound that is carried in the skins, stalks and pips of the grapes – to hold it together. But judging the right amount can be tricky. Too little and the wine will soften too soon, too much and it can taste tough or dried out. Currently many winemakers eliminate the harsher tannins that come from the stalks by de-stemming and rely instead on the more subtle effects they can obtain from oak ageing. Tannin can also be added in powdered form at the fermentation stage.

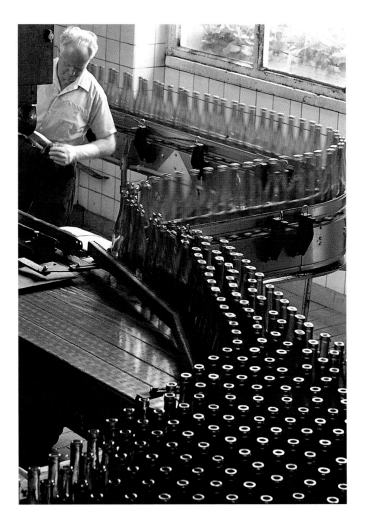

Above *A modern bottling line such as this ensures that the wine is bottled as quickly and hygienically as possible. Wine faults in the past were often caused by clumsy, dirty bottling. Since wine is now officially regarded as a food it is subject to much stricter hygiene controls.*

Far left *The finest wines will always spend some time ageing in oak barrels. They vary in size, but these 225-litre barriques made from new oak are the most popular. They are small enough to allow the wine to pick up the character of the oak.*

THE USE OF OAK

Most people have strong views about oak in wine which tend to be formed by their reaction to such notoriously oaky wines as Australian Chardonnay or Spanish Rioja. But, in fact, the presence of oak is not quite the black and white issue it might at first appear to be.

Originally wood had a perfectly straightforward function in relation to wine – that of a watertight container for storage and transport – but over the years winemakers discovered that the process of storage in wood not only had the bonus of naturally clarifying and stabilising wine but could affect its character, adding complex layers of flavour to white wines, and greater longevity and structure to reds. The degrees to which this happens depends on a number of factors.

Extent and manner of oak contact Wine can be stored in small barrels (in which case the oak influence will be more dominant) or in large oak casks. Alternatively, oak chips can be added to the wine during fermentation, either loose or encased in fabric, like an oversized tea bag.

Age of the container The barrels could be brand new or have been used only once or twice before. If an old oak cask is being used, its wood influence will be negligible. As you would expect, the newer the wood, the more powerful the oak flavour.

Type of oak Tight-grained French oak is still considered superior to any other kind of oak as it has a more subtle influence on the wine than vanilla-rich American oak – though the latter is often traditionally used for full-bodied reds such as Australian Shiraz and Rioja.

Degree of "toast" This is the extent to which the cooper (barrel maker) chars, or "toasts" the inside of the barrel. A moderate degree of toast will modify crude oak flavours.

Length of time in oak A wine can remain in the barrel for a few months or even years, but, also significant is whether the wine is actually fermented in the barrel. This technique is favoured for more expensive white wines as it gives them an opulent creamy texture and helps integrate the oak flavours.

Maturity of the wine when consumed Even with very oaky wines the influence of oak diminishes over time and its harsh tannins soften.

As important as any of these factors is the role of the winemaker him or herself. Certainly, wines of any quality will be assembled from a number of different components which may come from from different vineyards and be aged in different kinds of oak, for varying lengths of time. Part of the blend may, in fact, not have had any oak contact at all, but will have been aged in neutral stainless steel to accentuate its natural fruit.

With oak, as with other aspects of wine, you do generally get what you pay for. A white wine, for instance, costing £4 to 5 a bottle is going to show a much cruder oak influence than a fine burgundy matured in barrels made by a leading French cooper. Oak chips cost about one tenth the £300 to 400 a winemaker currently pays for a standard 225-litre oak barrel (a not unreasonable price when you consider that the wood is cut from trees that are at least 80 years old and may be seasoned for another two years before the cooper can use it). Although the quality of oak chips or, a more recent innovation, oak staves, can give a pleasant effect they are never going to achieve the sublimely creamy texture of wine aged in the best new oak barrels.

Certainly the fashion now is for far less overt oak character than was popular in the 1980s and early 1990s, with winemakers concentrating more on achieving balanced, integrated flavours with a greater degree of subtlety.

Oaked or unoaked?

Not all wines that are matured in oak taste obviously oaky. Most wines that are kept in old oak casks, including many fine white wines from Germany and Alsace, show no obvious flavour of the wood in which they are aged. Conversely, some wines such Sémillons from Australia and traditionally made full-bodied reds from the south of France, like Fitou, appear to be oaked when they haven't been anywhere near a barrel.

What to look for on the label

As oak is expensive winemakers who use it tend to boast about it. Descriptions such as "barrel matured" or "barrel fermented", "élevé en fûts de chêne" or the term "Reserva" or "Gran Reserva" indicate a significant oak influence. The back label may tell you how long the wine has been kept in oak, whether the oak is French or American, and how new the barrels are. Terms like "oak influenced" or "oak character" may indicate the use of chips rather than barrels.

Above A cooper "toasting" the staves of oak. This process, which helps bend the staves into the right shape, ultimately has a powerful effect on the flavour of the wine.

Far left The spectacular sight of a barrel cellar. The extensive financial investment involved in ageing wines in barrels inevitably results in some very expensive wines.

WINE STYLES EXPLAINED

Over the next 68 pages you'll find the heart of the book, the descriptions of the main wine styles. There are four white (crisp fresh dry; smooth, medium-bodied; rich, full-bodied; and aromatic and medium-dry) and four red (light fruity; smooth, medium-bodied; full-bodied; and aged wines and rarities). There are also sections for rosé, sparkling, sweet and fortified wines (sherry, port and Madeira). In each section you'll find an extensive listing of wines fitting that description. Each section is prefaced by an introduction highlighting the most important wines.

The starting point is to find the style of wine you like – for example crisp dry whites. Against each entry you'll find a series of symbols (with keys provided here and on the back cover) which tell you at a glance the main flavours in that wine, such as grassy, fruity and minerally. (These are listed in order so you can tell which flavour dominates.) You'll also find these symbols against other wines in other sections so if you like, for instance, spicy or oaky wines you'll be able to pick them out all the way through the book.

Also marked against each entry is a star rating which indicates the likely cost of the wine. It ranges from one star, which is the least expensive to three stars, which will be the dearest. Bear in mind that these are relative to the type of wine. A one star light, fruity red, for instance, will be a simple quaffing wine. A single star for champagne means it is inexpensive for champagne but obviously that doesn't make it cheap.

In most of the style sections you'll find a box headed **Starting Points**. These are suggestions of wines that you might like to try if you haven't drunk that type of wine before. They tend to be the most typical

Key to symbols

- Fruity
- Floral
- Minerally
- Spicy
- Nutty
- Grassy
- Toasty
- Oaky

| Crisp, fresh, dry whites | Smooth, medium-bodied whites | Rich, full-bodied whites | Aromatic and medium-dry whites |

examples of that wine style but they're also divided up to reflect the different options open to you. For example, in the aromatic whites section you can decide whether to experiment first with wines that are light and floral, fragrant and spicy or rich and aromatic.

There's also a section called **Label Clues**. These point out the key information you should look for on a label – for instance, references to the presence or absence of oak, the alcohol content (always a useful clue to a wine's weight and intensity) and the vintage.

By the side of the listings you'll find advice about storing and serving that particular style of wine which includes how long you should keep it, how long before you drink it you should open it, what temperature you should serve it and (where appropriate) the type of glasses you should serve it in. You'll find more general advice about storing and serving on pages 110–113. There's also an indication of the type of food and occasion for which that style of wine is most appropriate – or inappropriate. Again, you'll find more advice about matching food and wine in the section on Wine and Food (pages 104–109).

As you go through the book don't be surprised to find a wine in more than one section. Red burgundy, for example, can at its most basic be light and fruity, most is medium-bodied. Top burgundies such as Gevrey-Chambertin and Nuits-St-Georges count as full-bodied and *Grands Crus* like Romanée-Conti come into the category of aged wines and rarities. By and large, you will find these distinctions reflected in the price you pay. The more expensive the wine, the more intense and full-bodied it should be (though, maddeningly with burgundy, that isn't invariably the case).

Finally, there are always exceptions to the rule – some wines may differ slightly from their general discriptions in the listings. That's inevitable, however, as wine as a product is hugely varied. As in any other profession some winemakers are better at their job than others (or have better grapes to work with and a more reliable climate to work in) and wines do vary between one producer and another. You may initially find this a little frustrating – but discovering the unexpected is one of the great pleasures of wine drinking and what makes it so memorable!

| Light, fruity reds | Smooth, medium-bodied reds | Full-bodied reds | Aged wines & rarities | Rosé wines |

CRISP, FRESH, DRY WHITES

Dry is always a troublesome word in wine terms, for what is dry to one person may well not be so to another. For people accustomed to the tropical fruit of New World Chardonnay, Chablis would seem very dry. For someone brought up on Muscadet, it would taste quite full-bodied.

Nevertheless, there is a group of wines that ranges from bone dry whites such as Muscadet and Frascati to zesty New World Sauvignon that really couldn't be described as anything but dry. What these have in common is a crisp, tangy acidity that is in marked contrast to the smoother, rounded flavours of a Chardonnay or a wine made with oak.

Virtually all basic dry whites fall into this category, apart from those Germanic-style whites that have a distinctively floral, aromatic character (*see* page 54). The simple kind of quaffing wine you drink on holiday, the carafe wine in a restaurant, the cheapest whites on a supermarket shelf – all tend to be light, crisp, uncomplicated and fruity.

Most of them come from the Old World rather than the New. Hot climates tend to bring out richer, fruitier flavours than wines made in cooler more northerly regions. You would not find a wine like Muscadet or Vinho Verde in Australia. Chablis which is grown at virtually the same northerly latitude as the vineyards of the Loire has an altogether different character from a Chardonnay made in the Hunter Valley.

The style of many of these wines dates from when winemaking was much less sophisticated. Winemakers would use whatever local grapes were available and get the highest yields possible out of them, fashioning them in the most rudimentary way into simple quaffing wines that would be drunk on an everyday basis. In Italy, for example, local white wines such as Orvieto in Umbria and Frascati in Rome are still drunk with almost every kind of food, from pasta dishes right through to robustly flavoured stews.

Clean, modern wines

What has revolutionised this style of wine is modern vinification. It used to be impossible to make a fresh wine in a hot climate; the grapes would get too hot and the fermentation would take place at high temperatures producing yellow, oxidised wines. Now wines are made in immaculately clean, temperature-controlled stainless steel tanks. Almost any wine can be made to taste fresh, zesty and invigorating.

The most characterful wines in this style are undoubtedly those made from the Sauvignon Blanc grape which, like Chardonnay, has now spread from its traditional base in France to almost every wine-producing country in the world. Its style varies markedly from the delicate, racy gooseberry fruit of the Loire, to the more luscious rounded, juicy lime and pineapple fruit of Bordeaux (where it is often blended with Sémillon), to the soft citrus and apple flavours of California Fumé Blanc.

If you find such robust flavours not to your taste, there are plenty of alternatives. Italian grapes like Verdicchio and Vernaccia, better quality "Classico" versions of Orvieto and Soave (*see* Trebbiano entry), the rich, nutty quality of the best Muscadet *sur lie* or a fine, classically made unoaked Chablis can all provide a refreshing antidote to the sometimes over-exuberant ripe fruitiness of many New World wines.

One crucial thing to remember is that this type of crisp, fresh fruit fades fast. With the exception of the more expensive Sauvignons and of Chablis, the vast majority of bottles made in this style should be drunk as young as possible, within 12 months and in the case of cheaper wines within six. (Remember that southern hemisphere whites are six months ahead of European ones, typically arriving on the shelf in the autumn of the year they are harvested rather than the following spring.)

Label clues

"Dry White" should be an indication that a wine is precisely that, but sometimes wines labelled "dry" have an unexpectedly floral character. Check the back label for descriptions such as fragrant or aromatic (as opposed to crisp, fruity or citrussy). Wines that are described simply as "Blanc" (France), "Bianco" (Italy), "Blanco" (Spain), or "Branco" (Portugal) generally offer simple, fresh easy drinking.

Check the alcohol content of the wine – if you prefer a lighter style, look for wines of under 12 degrees. Finally, make sure that the wine comes from a recent vintage – the current or previous year for cheaper wines, not more than two years old for more expensive ones.

Above *Temperature-controlled stainless steel tanks have taken over from oak or cement casks for white wine fermentation, ensuring clean, fresh, fruity wines.*

Far left *The cool, high altitudes of much of northern Italy results in elegant, fresh flavours in the white wines.*

Starting points	
Minerally	**Fruity**
Italian Whites	Vin de Pays des Côtes de Gascogne
Muscadet	Inexpensive Bordeaux Sauvignon and
	Sauvignon de Touraine
Unoaked Chablis	South African Sauvignon
Sancerre	New Zealand Sauvignon

ALIGOTE

 Easily mistaken for Chardonnay, Aligoté is Burgundy's other white wine grape. However, except in the best vineyards in the best vintages, it can be uncomfortably sharp and rarely offers such good value as other wines from the region. It is also widely planted in Eastern Europe where it sometimes appears in blends with Chardonnay. ☆☆

BACCHUS, ORTEGA
and other English whites

 As in Germany, England's winemakers have been responding to the growing demand for dry, fruity whites. In the past, English wines were often made in a medium-dry style. Today most are clean and crisp. This has been helped by a move to newer grape varieties such as Bacchus, Ortega and Reichensteiner. Many are similar to a French Sauvignon, though some exhibit a more floral character. ☆☆

BADEN and other dry German whites

One of the few dry German wines, Baden comes from the south of Germany, a much warmer grape-growing area than the north. In fact, with German winemakers experimenting more with grape varieties such as Pinot Blanc (Weissburgunder) and Pinot Gris (Grauburgunder) there are more dry German wines than there used to be. Indications are the word "trocken" (dry) on the label, a square-shouldered Bordeaux style rather than the traditional flute-shaped bottle, or a New World type name like Northern Star. ☆→☆☆

BAIRRADA

The best-known Portuguese white after VINHO VERDE is a fresh, crisp, citrussy white. Cheaper versions are quite lemony, more expensive wines, more elegant and minerally. ☆→☆☆

BIANCO DI CUSTOZA

 Light, dry white from the Veneto in northeast Italy: clean and crisp with a touch of creaminess, but generally rather less exciting than neighbouring SOAVE. ☆→☆☆

CHABLIS

 The most obvious example of dry, crisp Chardonnay. Grand and Premier Cru Chablis may be full-bodied, but simple unoaked Chablis and **Petit Chablis** have a characteristically austere steely character, often evocatively described as flinty. ☆☆

CHARDONNAY

 This grape variety falls firmly within the next two style sections, but there are exceptions. Some white burgundy, notably those from younger vines, from a particularly cool area, or which are unoaked, can really taste quite tart and crisp. (CHABLIS and MACON BLANC.)

Any other Chardonnay grown in cool conditions will exhibit a similar character. For example there are a number of inexpensive Chardonnays produced in the Loire now under the label of **Vin de Pays du Jardin de la France**. They may be less lean than Chablis but they are crisp rather than smooth. ☆→☆☆

CHASSELAS

 Swiss grape variety used for bone dry white wines that are good with cooked cheese dishes like fondue. Rarely seen outside Switzerland, but certainly the wine to drink there. ☆☆

CHENIN BLANC – Loire Valley

 Although Chenin Blanc can acquire rich, honeyed tones with age, young Chenin, particularly in the cool Loire Valley in France, is often quite sharp. Quality varies from the rather dull wines of **Anjou** and **Saumur** (also made in medium-dry versions – *see* pages 54–59) to the austere, minerally elegance of **Savennières** and **Jasnières**. ☆→☆☆☆

ENTRE-DEUX-MERS

 Much improved appellation in the Bordeaux region of France producing prolific amounts of crisp, inexpensive, lemony whites, based on Sauvignon (though occasionally including some Sémillon and Muscadelle). ☆

FRASCATI

 The famous dry white wine of Rome, Frascati often used to be very light and dilute. Although these days those that find their way outside Italy are usually much fruitier. ☆→☆☆

GARGANEGA

 One of a number of indigenous Italian grape varieties (others are Catarrato, Grechetto,

Greco and Grillo) that are suddenly getting star billing on bottles. More characterful than TREBBIANO, with a delicate almond flavour, it features in wines like SOAVE and BIANCO DI CUSTOZA. ☆

GRUNER VELTLINER

 A popular grape variety in Austria and other countries in central and Eastern Europe, Grüner Veltliner is used to make fresh, young, sappy, whites with green apple and pepper flavours. Like Riesling, better quality wines can acquire more complex spicy, aromatic flavours over time (see pages 54–59). ☆

MACON BLANC

The most basic white wines from this southern part of Burgundy, made from the Chardonnay grape, can be quite light and acidic, particularly in a poor vintage when the grapes don't ripen fully. **Mâcon-Villages** (see page 46) is better value. ☆☆

MUSCADET

 A huge wine region in the Loire Valley producing bone dry, earthy, minerally whites that at their best are elegant, crisp and refreshing, at their (too frequent) worst, painfully thin and acidic. Quality, is however, slowly improving. The best wines tend to be those from the Sèvre-et-Maine part of the region and are labelled "sur lie" which have a richer, creamier flavour and texture. A similar style of wine, also from this region, is **Gros Plant**. ☆→☆☆

ORVIETO

 A lesser-known Italian white, from Umbria in central Italy, which tends to be more consistent than some of its rivals. Orvieto is clean and crisp with an appealing slightly earthy, nutty character, particularly in the higher-quality "Classico" wines. ☆→☆☆

PICPOUL DE PINET
and other southern French whites

 This is a crisp, fresh, minerally Muscadet-style white produced from the Picpoul grape near the Languedoc coast in southern France. Other whites in a similar style are produced in the area from grapes such as Roussanne, Grenache Blanc, Terret and Vermentino. You also find some crisp, dry whites in appellations such as **Corbières**, **Roussillon** and **Provence**. ☆

PINOT BIANCO

 The Italian name both for the Pinot Blanc grape and the wine made from it, mainly in the northeast of the country. It tends to be crisper and more acidic than French Pinot Blanc. ☆

PINOT GRIGIO

 An increasingly fashionable grape variety, grown mainly in northeast Italy where it produces characteristically dry, crisp, neutral-tasting whites. Some winemakers now manage to produce wines with a more pronounced fruit character, though they are never as rich or aromatic as wines labelled Pinot Gris (the alternative name of the grape). ☆→☆☆

Food and occasions

Crisp, fresh, whites are ideal for straightforward, everyday drinking, especially summer picnics and parties. They are perfect for drinking with salads or with grilled or barbecued fish and chicken. Muscadet has a great affinity with shellfish, while Chablis is the traditional partner for oysters. Italian whites are good with pasta, particularly made with seafood. Fruiter styles like Sauvignon go well with robustly flavoured fish dishes (though not generally those made with tomato), chicken and piquantly dressed salads. Delicate Loire Sauvignons work particularly well with asparagus, smoked salmon and goat's cheese while New Zealand Sauvignon is wonderful with Thai food.

RIOJA

White Rioja used to be heavily oaked and often oxidised from being left for months in oak barrels. Now a lighter, fresher style is popular. Most come from the Viura grape: light and fresh when unoaked, rounded, creamy and more Chardonnay-like when oaked. ☆→☆☆

RUEDA

One of Spain's most progressive wine regions which also gives its name to a crisp, fresh style of white based on the local Verdejo grape variety (with occasionally a little Sauvignon thrown in). Excellent value for money. ☆

SANCERRE & POUILLY-FUME

The best-known SAUVIGNONS from the Loire region in France, Sancerre and Pouilly-Fumé combine the characteristic gooseberry fruit with a pronounced grassiness, an aroma of currant leaves and a distinctive flinty, almost smoky character. They can also be intensely acidic, particularly in a difficult vintage. This leads to great variations in quality. The more powerful wines from top producers such as Dagueneau and de Ladoucette may contain some oak and belong in the full-bodied category (see pages 48–53). ☆☆→☆☆☆

SAUVIGNON BLANC

The Loire As with so many other wines, French Sauvignon provides the benchmark for the variety around the world. Its most distinctive manifestation are the elegant grassy gooseberryish wines from this region, notably SANCERRE and POUILLY-FUME, though better-value can be found from the lesser-known **Menetou-Salon**, **Quincy** and **Reuilly**, which tend to be more consistent, or from the cheaper but less complex **Sauvignon de Touraine** and **Sauvignon de Haut-Poitou**. ☆☆→☆☆☆

Bordeaux Sauvignon from this region and surrounding areas tends to be more citrussy and is often combined with Sémillon which gives it a roundness and softness that takes it out of this category. But crisp, fresh whites are produced by appellations such as ENTRE-DEUX-MERS, **Bergerac**, **Côtes de Duras** and simply as basic **Bordeaux Blanc**. ☆→☆☆

Languedoc Sauvignon is also widely planted throughout the Languedoc, a warmer region which gives it a richer, lime and lemon peel character. It is often produced as a varietal *vin de pays* (under the classification **Vin de Pays d'Oc**) and has more of a New World character than other French Sauvignons. ☆→☆☆

Other European Sauvignon No other European country produces such distinctive styles of Sauvignon as France, but most can boast one or two good examples. In Italy the most successful area for Sauvignon is Friuli in the northeast. In Spain it's RUEDA. In Austria, Styria. The large number of "flying winemakers" who have been working in Hungary has resulted in some powerfully flavoured wines, not subtle, but remarkable value for money. ☆→☆☆

New Zealand Sauvignon is the grape that has made New Zealand's reputation, and, indeed, the pungent version of the wine that it produces, with its rich gooseberry and tropical fruit, is as good as you'll find anywhere in the world. Many are so intense that they should more accurately be regarded as a full-bodied wine, though the chances are that if you enjoy other New World Sauvignons, you will also enjoy New Zealand's. The best examples come from the Marlborough region to the north of the South Island. They tend to be expensive, but are consistently reliable. ☆☆→☆☆☆

South Africa This country has proved expert at producing simple, inexpensive Sauvignon with intense, zesty fruit (usually with citrus rather than gooseberry flavours). But increasingly good producers – such as Bouchard Finlayson and Klein Constantia in the Constantia and Walker Bay areas are showing that they can produce world-class wines. ☆→☆☆☆

Chile Sauvignon from here tends to be softer and less assertive than that from New Zealand or South Africa, with a more delicate citrussy, grapefruit character. The best wines come from the Casablanca Valley, a well-favoured, cool, coastal region which produces wines of considerable elegance and style. ☆→☆☆

California Californians actually prefer their Sauvignon softer and less acid, hence the popularity of Fumé Blanc (see pages 42–47). But there are Sauvignons made in the more usual crisp, citrussy style. If you prefer that style look out for wines that are labelled Sauvignon rather than Fumé Blanc. ☆☆

Australia Although a bit hot to be ideal Sauvignon growing territory, Australia does have producers who do it successfully, particularly in cooler areas such as the Adelaide Hills. The resulting wines tend to be quite intensely flavoured, often with a pronounced lemon peel character. ☆☆

SOAVE

Another very much improved wine from the Veneto in northeast Italy. You still find some dreary examples about, but at its best, Soave has a distinctive, delicate almondy flavour that makes it an attractive partner for food. Wines labelled "Classico" could equally well fall into the next section (*see* pages 42–47). ☆→☆☆

TREBBIANO

A rather unexciting, neutral grape variety that has traditionally been the backbone of many dry Italian whites, accounting for their strong family resemblance. But improved winemaking methods have given it a new lease of life and it increasingly features on labels in its own right, both in Italy and in Australia where it makes perfectly decent clean, fruity whites. ☆

VERDICCHIO DEI CASTELLI DI JESI

The best-known wine made from the Verdicchio grape, this romantic sounding wine from the eastern side of Italy has an attractively fresh, tangy, slightly lemony flavour. It frequently comes in a distinctive, curvy bottle. ☆☆

VERNACCHIA DI SAN GIMIGNANO

Made around the famous hillside town just outside Florence from the local Vernacchia grape. Like VERDICCHIO, it still tends to be made the traditional way, resulting in a a crisp fresh white not unlike a MUSCADET. ☆☆

VINHO VERDE

Portugal's best-known white wine. Most is very light in alcohol, quite sharp and with a slight spritz: the kind of wine you enjoy on holiday, but which doesn't always translate into good drinking back home. Estate bottled versions are more interesting, particularly those made from the Alvarinho grape. ☆

VINOS DE LA TIERRA

The Spanish equivalent to the French *vin de pays*, this is a relatively new category of wine which should provide simple, dry white wines of rather better quality than some of the rather dull, commercial offerings of regions like **La Mancha** and **Valencia**. ☆

VIN DE PAYS DES COTES DE GASCOGNE

The most consistently reliable of French *vins de pays*, Vin de Pays des Côtes de Gascogne, which comes from southwest France, provides fresh, fruity, uncomplicated drinking. A *vin de pays* is almost always a better buy these days than a simple *vin blanc*. ☆

Storing and serving

Serve chilled (at least an hour in the fridge). Drink as soon as possible after you buy it, within six months for cheaper wines, and two years for the best wines in this category.

SMOOTH, MEDIUM-BODIED DRY WHITES

If someone wanted to learn about wine and asked you where they should start, you'd probably point them to a smooth, dry white. Not too sharp or acidic, not too intimidatingly oaky, not too floral or sweet, white wine like this is the perfect starting point to begin your exploration of the wine world.

In fact, the chances are you wouldn't direct them to just any smooth, dry white wine, you'd pour them a glass of Chardonnay. Chardonnay is the wine that more than any other dominates this section. The one you'll find most often on the supermarket shelf, the one you'll find in restaurants, there is a literally a world of Chardonnay to choose from.

So what distinguishes Chardonnay that is made in this style from the more fuller-flavoured kind? As is explained earlier in the book, it's primarily a question of the climate the vines are grown in and whether or not the resulting wine is oaked (*see* pages 32–33). On the whole you'll find that Chardonnay grown in cooler, more northerly regions such as Burgundy and northern Italy, or in cooler parts of warmer countries like Chile, will be lighter and creamier than Chardonnay produced in hot countries like Australia or South Africa, or warmer areas like the Languedoc in the south of France.

Subtle use of oak

Chardonnay made in this style may well be oaked, but it doesn't have the obvious oaky character of, say, a top California Chardonnay or an expensive white burgundy. Apart from the inherent quality of the grapes themselves, it could be due to the fact that the wine is not made in brand new oak barrels, that the barrels are made out of French rather than American oak, or that it only spends a relatively short time in barrel – or in contact with oak chips (*see* pages 32–33). But even among wines made in this style, they can and will vary. Ageing a small proportion of the wine in oak (10 or 15 per cent), will give it a smoother, richer character than that of a completely unoaked Chardonnay.

In the absence of obvious clues from the winemaker, such as putting "barrel-fermented" on the label, the best guide to style is price. It is not a totally hard and fast rule because producers in countries with low production costs like Argentina, Spain or South Africa may produce a big oaky wine that is comparatively cheap. But it's true to say that most inexpensive or moderately priced Chardonnays will be lighter and fruitier in style than expensive ones. This is particularly true of wines that are produced by the world's biggest wine producing companies.

Well-known brands like Lindeman's Bin 65 or Gallo's Turning Leaf Chardonnay that sell to literally hundreds of thousands of people are deliberately made in a smoothly fruity, easy-drinking style.

Chardonnay apart, where else within this style should you pursue your wine drinking adventures? Well, it depends on your personal preference. If you like a lighter, more creamy style of wine you should try something like a South African Chenin Blanc or the delicately peachy flavours of an Oregon Pinot Gris. If you prefer something slightly sweeter-tasting you might consider a Colombard or the classic Australian blend of Sémillon and Chardonnay with its exuberant, ripe pineapple fruit.

If you're looking for more distinctive flavours you're more likely to find them in the Old World. White Bordeaux which is much less well-known than its red counterpart, offers beautifully elegant drinking and is often excellent value for money. Alsace Pinot Blanc is an underrated treasure. Italy has more to offer than the simple Soaves and Frascatis you find in the typical *trattoria*. Show you're in the know by ordering a smooth, creamy Lugana or the incredibly chic Gavi.

Finally, don't make the mistake of thinking that just because these wines are slightly more expensive than the simple, everyday quaffing wines that were described in the last section, that you can store them away for years. Almost all modern wines now are meant to be drunk young and this style of wine is no exception.

Label clues

Scan the back-label for clues about how the wine is made. Expressions like "lightly oaked" or "left on its lees" indicate a lighter style. Mention of barrel fermentation or up to a year in oak means the wine belongs in the next section. Look out for an alcohol content of 12–13 degrees.

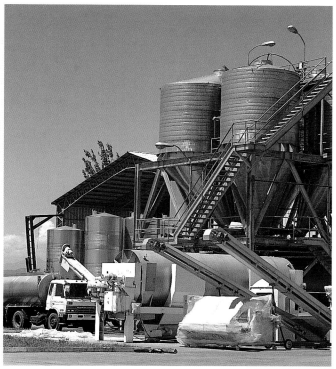

Above *Australia is a significant contributor to this style of wine with many soft, ripe, creamy wines, primarily made from Chardonnay.*

Far left *Bordeaux produces some of the finest examples of this style. The best wines are lush and smooth and have a delicious subtle peachiness.*

Starting points	
Drier	**Fruitier**
Inexpensive or moderately priced white burgundy	Unoaked Australian Chardonnay
Alsace Pinot Blanc	Pays d'Oc Chardonnay
South African Chenin Blanc	South African Chardonnay
Chilean Chardonnay	Sémillon-Chardonnay
	New World Colombard

BORDEAUX BLANC

While basic white Bordeaux is simple, crisp and fruity, wines from this region that are oaked take on a much more lush, smooth, peachy quality. This is mainly due to the fact that they are not pure Sauvignon Blanc but a blend of Sauvignon and SEMILLON (and occasionally Muscadelle) and Sémillon has a particular affinity with oak. The best known white Bordeaux is **Graves** – though the top quality wines now come from the breakaway appellation of **Pessac-Léognan** (*see* page 48–53). ☆☆→☆☆☆

BOURGOGNE BLANC

Basic white burgundy (Appellation Bourgogne Blanc) is highly variable in quality. At its worst it can be dull and characterless, but at its best it is attractively light and creamy. Producers who also include the word Chardonnay on the label are likely to make their wine in a more typically fruity New World style. ☆☆

BURGUNDY

White burgundy in general has a quite distinctive character that traditionally has little in common with New World CHARDONNAY, though several producers are now making their wines in a more obviously New World style. The fruit flavours are much less obvious, peach or apricot rather than mango and pawpaw, but above all, the feel of the wine in your mouth is different. There's a rich creamy, slightly oily texture to burgundy that you rarely find anywhere else and which becomes more pronounced as the wine gets older. (Unlike most inexpensive and medium priced New World Chardonnays, white burgundy will age for several years.)

Most of the wines in this price range and style come from the Mâconnais and Côte Chalonnaise regions (MACON and MONTAGNY), rather than the more prestigious Côte de Beaune (*see* pages 48–53). Wines that are made by individual growers, even given quite humble labels like BOURGOGNE BLANC, are generally better quality than wines from the big *négociants* and cooperatives. ☆☆→☆☆☆

CHABLIS

Although Chablis, which is to the north of the BURGUNDY region is traditionally steely-dry (*see* pages 36–41) the region's producers are increasingly responding to the demand from wine drinkers for smoother, less acidic wines. Much standard Chablis is now made in this style, though wines labelled Premier or Grand Cru (which, unlike most basic Chablis, are aged in oak) will be more full-bodied (*see* pages 48–53). ☆☆→☆☆☆

CHARDONNAY

Pays d'Oc Chardonnay The huge sprawling Languedoc region in the south of France has become a playground for overseas (particularly Australian) winemakers and many of the Chardonnays from the region reflect that fruitier New World style. That is specially likely with wines that are given New World style names like "Southlands", or where the name Chardonnay is prominent on the label: usually alongside the appellation

Vin de Pays d'Oc. Chardonnay produced around the cooler Limoux region to the north of the Languedoc is generally lighter and more Burgundian in style. ☆→☆☆

Bulgaria, Hungary and Moldova Flying winemakers are also much in evidence in this part of the world producing simple, smooth, lightly oaked Chardonnays that offer exceptionally good value for money. Wines that are described as barrel or barrique-fermented will be fuller-bodied. ☆

Italy The most inexpensive Italian Chardonnay is produced in the north of country in the Alto Adige, Trentino, Fruili and the Veneto to the east, and Piedmont to the west. When unoaked it tends to be quite light, crisp and lemony, when oaked much like mid-price Chardonnay from any other cool wine region. Names to look out for are **Chardonnay delle Venezie** (or Tre Venezie), **Chardonnay del Trentino** and **Chardonnay del Piemonte**. For a fuller style try **Chardonnay del Salento** from Puglia down in the south. ☆→☆☆

New World Chardonnay Most moderately priced New World Chardonnay is made in a smooth, medium-bodied style. The difference between them lies in how fruity or how oaky they are. The lighter, more citrussy ones tend to come from Chile, the more fruity from South Africa or Australia, the oakiest from California, New Zealand and the more expensive bottles from Australia and South Africa (*see* pages 48–53). Wines to look out for are the increasingly popular unoaked or unwooded Chardonnays which tend to have a particularly fresh peachy or melony flavour without the marked oak character that some drinkers find unappealing. ☆→☆☆

CHARDONNAY BLENDS

 Blends of Chardonnay with other grape varieties are increasingly popular and the style obviously varies depending on which grape it is blended with. Blends with less expensive varieties such as CHENIN BLANC, VIURA or with obscure Eastern European grapes like Rikat or Zenit can result in lighter wines. Blends with varieties with a more dominant personality like COLOMBARD and SEMILLON will produce much fruitier, fuller-flavoured wines. ☆→☆☆

CHENIN BLANC

 Chenin grown in the New World tends not to have the same tart acidity as that from the Loire Valley in France. Most comes from South Africa where it produces smooth, melony whites, often with a touch of sweetness. Some winemakers, though, are experimenting with barrel-fermentation or leaving the young wine on its lees, resulting in wines with a fuller, creamier texture. Wines labelled "Bush Vine" (coming from older vines), also tend to be rather more stylish and elegant.

Chenin is also quite widely grown by wine producers in California, Chile and Argentina with similar results. Blends with other grapes such as CHARDONNAY, Sauvignon and COLOMBARD take on the characteristics of those more dominant varieties. ☆

COLOMBARD

 Australian Colombard has a particularly ripe, tropical fruity character that makes it easily mistaken for CHARDONNAY – with which it is often blended. But it doesn't quite have Chardonnay's subtlety of flavour or smooth creamy texture and can frequently taste almost sweet. It is also widely planted in South Africa where it is used to make inexpensive fruity whites, again often blended with Chardonnay or CHENIN BLANC. ☆

COTES DU RHONE

 White Côtes du Rhône is much less well-known than red, but in the right hands can produce a smooth, dry, slightly nutty white that can make a refreshing change from New World varietals. ☆→☆☆

FUME BLANC

 Fumé Blanc was an ingenious name cooked up by the California wine producer Robert Mondavi for Sauvignon Blanc, whose green herbaceous flavours the Californians have never really developed a taste for. Nowadays, the name has become synonymous with the particular style of Sauvignon pioneered by Mondavi which is generally lightly oaked and therefore softer, less acidic and more appley than French or other New World Sauvignons. It is still a style favoured more by Americans than elsewhere in the wine world, though occasionally other producers do crop up with a Sauvignon made in the "Fumé" style. ☆→☆☆

GAILLAC

 A soft, spicy, slightly appley white from the southwest of France made from the local Mauzac grape variety. ☆

Food and occasions

This style of wine is infinitely adaptable: it goes with a wide range of different dishes and fits into almost any occasion. Lighter styles go well with fish, chicken and pasta, particularly if accompanied by a creamy sauce. A good quality wine like a white burgundy will accompany a rich fish like salmon or a classic roast chicken. Fruitier styles can take slightly spicier flavours. A good style of wine for informal entertaining.

GAVI

An extremely fashionable, elegant, dry white wine from the Piedmont region of northern Italy whose price is often well out of proportion to its quality. (The worst culprits are producers that call their wines Gavi di Gavi.) A better bargain can be wines labelled **Cortese** which is the grape that is used to make Gavi. ☆☆→☆☆☆

LUGANA

Another stylish and occasionally pricey Italian white from Lombardy to the south of Lake Garda in northern Italy, with a creamy delicately nutty, subtle flavour. It is similar to a good quality SOAVE CLASSICO and generally a much more reliable choice when ordering off a restaurant wine list. ☆☆

MACON-VILLAGES

Wines from the Mâconnais region to the north of Beaujolais are generally fuller flavoured than CHABLIS, though again, they can vary in quality. Wines labelled Mâcon-Villages or which come from individual villages in the region like **Mâcon-Lugny** or **Mâcon-Viré** are likely to be more rewarding than basic **Mâcon Blanc**. ☆☆

MARSANNE
and other southern French whites

Although many of the New World style whites produced in the south of France are made from widely planted grape varieties like CHARDONNAY and Sauvignon, the favoured style of the Languedoc-Roussillon was traditionally drier and more earthy than the fruity styles that are popular now. Wines made from Marsanne and Roussanne (grapes also grown in the Rhône) are more likely to be in this style, as are some of the more individual wines produced by small producers in **Corbières** or **Roussillon** or under the catch-all appellation **Coteaux du Languedoc**. ☆→☆☆

MONTAGNY

A white wine appellation in the Côte Chalonnaise which is increasingly going over to the use of new oak barrels and producing wines in a more obviously oaky style. Other lesser-known appellations that offer good value for money in this part of BURGUNDY are **Mercurey** and **Rully**. ☆☆

PINOT BLANC

Pinot Blanc, the same grape as Italy's Pinot Bianco, on the whole produces smooth, dry, neutrally flavoured whites without any great distinction. The main exception is Alsace in France which has evolved a far more elegant and creamy style, not dissimilar from a lighter style of CHARDONNAY. Some impressive Pinot Blanc is also produced in Austria and Germany under the name **Weissburgunder**. ☆☆

PINOT GRIS – North America

The ABC (Anything But Chardonnay) tendency is very taken at the moment with Pinot Gris: a grape that can be fashioned into a smooth stylish peachy-apricotty white, with crisper acidity than its ubiquitous rival. It is particularly popular in Oregon but there are also producers showing an interest in California, Canada and New York State. ☆☆

RUEDA

Although Spain's Rueda is increasingly been made in a crisper style, the traditional style of the wine – which you may still encounter among smaller producers is softer and more appley. ☆→☆☆

RIOJA

White Rioja used invariably to be an intense, full-bodied, slightly sherried wine and some producers still make it that way (*see* pages 100–101). Most Spanish winemakers these days have cast aside their old oak barrels in favour of new oak and are making it in a much lighter, fruitier style. Unlike traditional white Rioja, new style Rioja is best drunk young: look for the most recent vintage. ☆→☆☆

ST-VERAN

This is a village within the MACON appellation in the south of BURGUNDY which generally produces good value wines with an attractively rich, creamy texture. It is often referred to as poor man's **Pouilly-Fuissé** (its more famous neighbouring wine) which spends longer in oak and generally has a fuller style (*see* pages 48–53). ☆☆

SEMILLON

Sémillon appears in so many guises that it's hard to pin a typical style down. Nevertheless, most Sémillon that appears on its own as a varietal, with the significant exception of the majority of Australian Sémillons, are made in this style. Having said that, there isn't very much of it outside Australia: a little in Chile, the odd drop from New Zealand, some from Washington State. In all these places it makes pleasantly smooth, fruity wines but generally without the exciting depth of flavour you find in Australia. ☆→☆☆

SEMILLON/CHARDONNAY

"Sém/Chard" as it's jocularly known in the trade is a popular duo that features in a number of Australia's more inexpensive brands. Fruitier than CHARDONNAY on its own, less rich and full-bodied than straight Australian Sémillon (*see* pages 48–53), it provides attractively uncomplicated, fruity drinking. Chardonnay lovers may find it a little sweet, but, nevertheless, these wines provide a good starting point for newcomers to wine. ☆→☆☆

SICILY

Produced much further south than most Italian whites, Sicilian whites have always been rather more full-bodied, but the introduction of modern winemaking techniques by visiting winemakers and inspired use of the local grape varieties like Catarratto, Grecanico, Grillo and Inzolia have resulted in some really characterful fruity whites. An up-and-coming area that should continue to offer exceptionally good value for money. ☆

SOAVE CLASSICO

So much basic Soave in the past has been bland and flavourless that it might seem too light a wine to appear in this section. But the better quality wines, usually labelled "Classico", have an attractive creamy texture and a delicate almondy flavour. ☆☆

VERDELHO

A grape, traditionally used for the production of Madeira, which has been given a new lease of life, particularly by winemakers in Australia. The resulting wines are juicy and refreshing with an appealing limey fruitiness. ☆☆

VIURA

The Spanish grape that has always been the backbone of white RIOJA is now getting a chance to star on its own. Oaked versions have a pleasingly light, creamy flavour. ☆

Storing and serving

Drink lightly chilled (no longer than an hour in the fridge). Chilling this style of wine too much can dull its delicate flavours. Drink more inexpensive bottles within about three months. A better quality wine like a Chablis or St-Veran will keep much longer, though it may lose something of its initial freshness.

RICH, FULL-BODIED WHITES

A few years ago, when the fashion for big oaky Chardonnays was at its height, you would have found more wines in this section. That was when every winemaker wanted to copy the full-bodied, tropical fruity style that had proved so popular in California and Australia. Now the pendulum has swung back. Just as people are increasingly turning to a lighter style of food, they're looking for lighter, more refreshing wines.

So where does that leave Chardonnay? As mentioned in the previous section, it has now has a foot firmly in both camps. Most inexpensive and moderately priced Chardonnays are now made in a lighter, smoother style, while more expensive ones tend to be rich and full-bodied. (Why give customers lashings of expensive oak for nothing if they're equally happy without it?)

The chief characteristics of these fuller Chardonnays – for it is this grape that again dominates this section – are concentration and complexity. This comes partly from the careful selection of vineyards. The New World has discovered what the Old World has known for years, the importance of *terroir* – the unique configuration of situation, soil and climate that makes one site so much better than another. Increasingly, Californian and Australian wines indicate a more specific area of origin: not just Napa but Carneros, not southeast Australia but the Clare or Barossa Valleys or Padthaway.

The winemaker's mixing palette

A show-piece Chardonnay may have as many as five or six components including wines from different sites, some unoaked, some barrel fermented, some fermented in stainless steel but then put into barrels which could be brand new, one or two years old or lightly or more heavily charred. As a result, the winemaker can build up a complex palette of flavours: vanilla oak gives way to cream, mango to apricot, grapefruit and lime, simple sweetness to refreshing acidity with oak blending in seamlessly to give an overall richness and a long, lingering finish.

The result is that it's now more difficult to tell top Chardonnays apart. On the whole, those from the New World will be a little sweeter, a little smoother, richer and more buttery, but they can vary; professional tasters can and do get it wrong. Where they still differ is in their capacity to age. Even the best New World examples age less seductively, developing a rather heavy, slightly cloying character, instead of the rich nuttiness and thrilling acidity of the best white burgundy. You'd drink most top Californian or Australian Chardonnay within three to five years. Your Montrachet or Corton-Charlemagne could easily survive 20.

Longevity is also a feature of the other top wines of this section. Wines like Hermitage and the classed-growths of Bordeaux such as those of Pessac-Léognan create extraordinarily opulent, complex wines which, in the best vintages, will last several decades.

More affordable versions of both, albeit of a different character, can be found in Australia. The Marsanne grape on which Hermitage is based and Sémillon, the basis of white Bordeaux (with Sauvignon Blanc) both star on their own Down Under. When young they taste like any other fruity Australian white, but after a few years both develop the most marvellous rich pineapple and dried fruit flavours. And because neither is particularly fashionable they offer excellent value for money.

To sum up, these are generally not the kind of wines you'd drink everyday. Most are too expensive, too rich and heavy or too quirky. Save them for special occasions and for people you know are going to enjoy the experience as much as you will: the kind of meal where the wine comes first, then you wonder what you're going to eat with it.

Label clues

Most of these wines will be high in alcohol: 13–13.5 degrees (Australian Sémillons and Marsannes may be lower). Check the vintage. A wine older than three years may not be as fresh and fruity as you're used to, but it may be more complex. Look at the back-label to see how long the wine has spent in oak: more than 12 months and it is likely to have a more pronounced, oaky character.

Starting points	
European style Chardonnay	**Anything but Chardonnay**
Fine white burgundy	Australian Sémillon
California Chardonnay	Australian Marsanne
(Carneros)	Traditional white Rioja
New World Chardonnay	Pessac-Léognan (Graves)
South African Chardonnay	
Australian Chardonnay	
New Zealand Chardonnay	

Above *The pretty Burgundian village of Pernand-Vergelesses nestles alongside the vineyard of Corton-Charlemagne – the source of one of the world's most highly prized white wines.*

Far left *The Hunter Valley in Australia is producing slightly more subtle styles of Chardonnay than were previously popular. The wines are big, nevertheless, but with a little less oak and more complexity of flavour.*

BURGUNDY

 There is no white wine as opulently sensual as an expensive white burgundy, the finest expression of the CHARDONNAY grape. The extraordinary interplay of flavours: butter, cream, hazelnuts, peach, lime, the odd hint of cinnamon spice, make it a once-tried-never-forgotten experience. This complexity takes time to evolve. Few wines of this class are ready to drink before they are three years old and may continue to improve until they are eight or 10. The effect of age changes the wines' character, making them less creamy, softer, richer and more honeyed, with even a slightly oily or vegetal character that you may or may not like.

Burgundy's vineyards can be difficult to get a grip on because of the multiplicity of different names. Most growing areas have wines that are labelled Premier Cru or Grand Cru which come from specific parcels of land which were singled out during the last century as producing wines of the highest quality. Grand Cru (theoretically at least) signifies the finest wines, Premier Cru the next best, but the very finest examples undoubtedly come from tiny production areas like CORTON-CHARLEMAGNE.

Unfortunately, not all burgundy hits these giddy heights so it does repay buying from a specialist – or a sommelier who knows his wine list well. Be suspicious of wines of this reputation that are offered at well below the normal price.

Lesser-known white burgundies in this style which can offer particularly good value for money are **Auxey-Duresses**, **Pernand-Vergelesses**, **St-Aubin** and **St-Romain**. These villages are well worth looking out for. ☆☆☆

CHABLIS GRAND CRU

 Although basic Chablis is dry and flinty, the top quality wines, which are labelled Grand Cru fall firmly in this category. They include Blanchot, Bougros, Les Clos, Grenouilles, Les Preuses, Valmur and Vaudésir. Some Premier Cru wines could be classified as full-bodied, though there are now so many of them (they account for about a quarter of the region's wines) that many are frankly not a great deal better than basic Chablis.

Given some bottle age, Chablis develops powerful, rich, almost tropical flavours – quite different from the lean steely quality of its youth. Grand Cru Chablis shouldn't be drunk for at least five years and can age magnificently for 10 years or even longer. ☆☆☆

CHARDONNAY – oak aged

Europe (excluding France) Most European Chardonnays are made in a lighter style than this. The exception is Spain which, in the up-and-coming regions of Navarra and Somantano, is producing some impressively toasty, full-bodied Chardonnays at a very reasonable price. There are also a few individual winemakers with ambitions to make serious, top-quality Chardonnay – with prices to match. Examples are Gaja, Antinori and Avignonesi in Italy, Domaine Constantin in Greece and Miguel Torres, whose highly regarded Milmanda is produced in the Conca de Barbera region of Spain. ☆→☆☆☆.

California There may have been a reaction against Chardonnay among the cognoscenti (witness the Anything But Chardonnay movement) but most North American wine drinkers, and winemakers, still take the variety very seriously. Nowhere is that more the case than in California which by common consent makes the highest quality white wines outside Burgundy. The heart of Chardonnay production is the Napa Valley, particularly at the cooler southern end, Carneros where top producers such as Cuvaison and Saintsbury have their vineyards. Other favoured areas are Sonoma (particularly the Russian River Valley). Some exciting Chardonnay is also produced to the south of San Francisco in Monterey County, and in the Edna and Santa Maria Valleys of the Central Coast. ☆☆→☆☆☆

Canada This country has advanced by leaps and bounds as a Chardonnay producer in recent years and now turns out some weightily impressive wines. Most of these come from the Ontario region. ☆☆→☆☆☆

New York State Just over the border from Ontario, the wines of New York State are very similar in character. Some quite CHABLIS-like examples come from producers in Long Island and around the Finger Lakes. ☆☆→☆☆☆

Pacific Northwest (Oregon and Washington State) So far Washington has the edge over Oregon as a Chardonnay producer, creating richly fruity full-bodied Chardonnays in a typically Californian style. But Oregon's wines could turn out in the longer term to be a closer approximation to BURGUNDY's, particularly as some of the smaller producers adopt more traditional methods. ☆☆→☆☆☆

Australia Just as everybody thought they knew where they were with Australian Chardonnay, the goalposts have moved. The big walloping oaky style of the late 1980s and early 1990s has fallen out of fashion in favour of much more restrained wines: not burgundy certainly, but Chardonnay that often shows a creamily elegant character and a much fresher acidity than in the past. The most prized vineyards are now those in cooler areas: the Clare and Eden Valleys, Padthaway, and the Adelaide Hills in South Australia and the Yarra Valley in Victoria. Even in the hot, humid Hunter Valley there is a new region called Orange that looks particularly promising for Chardonnay. Wines that are made in Western Australia, too, are far removed from the stereotype. Chardonnays from such top producers as Cullen, Leuwin and Moss Wood can hold their own with the world's best. Make no mistake, these are still big wines, but they are altogether more serious than the simple, uncomplicated fruit-and-oak recipe Chardonnays we're used to. ☆☆ → ☆☆☆

New Zealand It's ironic that New Zealand is best-known for its Sauvignon when its Chardonnay is so fine. The economics of the industry here mean that very few inexpensive wines are produced, which justifies generous expenditure on good quality oak barrels. There are detectable regional differences: Chardonnays from the Gisborne and Hawkes Bay areas on the North Island show a more obviously tropical fruit character than those from the cooler Marlborough region of the South Island. As with Australia though, there are significant differences within regions too. The Wairarapa area to the south of the North Island, for example, produces a classically creamy Burgundian style of Chardonnay. Overall though, expect big full-bodied wines with a noticeable oak influence, in a style that falls somewhere between those of Australia and California. ☆☆ → ☆☆☆

South Africa Although most inexpensive Chardonnays fall within the previous style section, South Africa is also one of the cheapest producers of a more full-bodied style – albeit that the oak can be pretty obvious. There is also an increasing number of more expensive Chardonnays being produced by such producers as Neil Ellis, Hamilton Russell, Klein Constantia, Thelema and Vergelegen which, while they have yet to reach the standard of the best the New World has to offer, are certainly within sight of it. ☆☆

Chile Only Chile's top ranking Reserva Chardonnays are full-bodied enough to fall into this section, but they too are on the increase. Like so many of Chile's wines, they offer good value for money. ☆☆

Argentina This country is now approximately where Chile was about five years ago with regard to white winemaking. Chardonnays therefore tend to be very obviously oaky, but have the virtue of being extremely good value. ☆ → ☆☆

CORTON-CHARLEMAGNE

Fabulously lush creamy, buttery Grand Cru from the village of Aloxe-Corton to the north of the CÔTE DE BEAUNE that can take several years to reveal its true magnificence. Unusually for white BURGUNDY, a proportion of Pinot Blanc and Pinot Gris may be included. Very scarce and very expensive. ☆☆☆

Food and occasions

These fuller-bodied whites can be partnered by equally richly flavoured food. Save fine whites from Bordeaux and Burgundy and the best New World Chardonnays for special occasions and lavish ingredients like turbot and lobster. More inexpensive wines like Australian Chardonnays and Sémillons go well with a modern European or slightly spicy Pacific Rim style of cooking.

COTE DE BEAUNE

Most of BURGUNDY's top whites (apart from CHABLIS) come from the Côte de Beaune – a favoured piece of land which produces the region's greatest whites and some of its most prestigious reds. The fabulous prices they command stem from there being very limited quantities available. Wines labelled "Côte de Beaune", however, will be considerably lighter. ☆☆→☆☆☆☆

JURANCON SEC

An obscure but delightful curiosity, this elegant, dry, spicy, full-bodied wine is made in the southwest of France near the Pyrenees. It also has a delicious sweet counterpart (see pages 92–97). ☆☆☆

MARSANNE

This grape variety is the unsung hero of white wines from the RHONE but its main claim to fame is the varietal wines it makes in a very specific area of Australia, Victoria's Goulbourn Valley. There two producers, Chateau Tahbilk and Mitchelton produce some remarkably deep coloured wines with rich baked pineapple-grilled grapefruit flavours which, like SEMILLON, are at their most impressive after several years' ageing. ☆☆

MEURSAULT

The largest wine commune of the fabled COTE DE BEAUNE producing big, full-bodied CHARDONNAYS with a rich butterscotch, toasty

oak character. Although there are no Grands Crus in this commune, most wines are full-bodied. One of the more widely available of the top white burgundies and a reasonably reliable buy on wine lists. ☆☆→☆☆☆☆

PESSAC-LEOGNAN (GRAVES)

What most people still think of as Graves, Bordeaux's most famous dry white wine, these days is more likely to come from the more recently established region of Pessac-Léognan. This region managed to walk away with most of the prizes when the Graves appellation was split up. This is SEMILLON and SAUVIGNON at their finest: graceful, elegant, creamy, with the capacity to age for many years – even decades – and an ideal refuge for wine enthusiasts looking for alternatives to CHARDONNAY. ☆☆→☆☆☆☆

POUILLY-FUISSE

The most famous of the white wines from the Mâconnais (see **Mâcon** page 46). Like CHABLIS the quality is particularly uneven. There are no Premier or Grand Cru wines: the best come from single vineyards and consistently reliable producers such as Ferret, Guffens-Heynen and Marcel Vincent at Château Fuissé. ☆☆→☆☆☆☆

PULIGNY-MONTRACHET & CHASSAGNE- MONTRACHET

Two villages to the south of the COTE DE BEAUNE which at their best produce some of the most seductively elegant and creamy

of all white BURGUNDIES. The finest of all come from individual Grand Cru vineyards like **Le Montrachet** and **Bâtard-Montrachet** which span the two growing areas. But the very limited size of these (Bâtard-Montrachet has 12 hectares, Le Montrachet eight and **Bienvenues-Bâtard-Montrachet** only four) ensures that these wines remain the province of millionaire wine collectors. Puligny and Chassagne-Montrachet are more affordable but still by no means cheap. ☆☆→☆☆☆☆

RHONE – whites

It has to be said that the great white wines of the Rhône are something of an acquired taste. In their youth they have a very dry, slightly oily, sherried sort of flavour and can take years to open up to the point where they become magnificent. The best known is **Hermitage**, a third of whose production is devoted to whites based on the classic Rhône grapes MARSANNE and Roussanne, but other Rhône appellations better known for their reds like **Châteauneuf-du-Pape**, **Crozes-Hermitage** and **St-Joseph** also produce a limited number of white wines.

There is already evidence that producers in the region are making their wines more consumer-friendly which looks likely to make the Rhône a rewarding source of top quality whites in the years to come. ☆☆→☆☆☆☆

RIOJA – traditional whites

Although the fashion in Rioja is now for much fresher whites, you can still find examples of wines made in a more traditional style. Aged for up to four years in big oak casks, they acquire a slightly baked, oxidised flavour that is at odds with many modern wine drinkers' tastes though they are one of the few alternatives to CHARDONNAY at this level of drinking. Wines labelled "Crianza" (which are aged for a minimum of six months) are likely to be lighter than those labelled "Reserva" or "Gran Reserva" which have to be aged for two and four years respectively. ☆☆

SAUVIGNON BLANC

While most Sauvignon tastes light, fresh and crisp in the top growing areas of the Loire Valley (Sancerre and Pouilly Fumé) and in the Marlborough region of New Zealand, it can produce rich intensely flavoured wines that are heavyweight by anyone's standards. Usually that means that a proportion of the wine has been oaked (as is the case with New Zealand's fabled Cloudy Bay), that it has been left on its lees to develop extra flavour (see pages 26–31), or that it contains an small amount of SEMILLON.

Some top French, Californian and Italian producers also make Sauvignon in this style, such as Châteaux Margaux's Pavillon Blanc or Gaja's Alteni di Brassica. ☆☆→☆☆☆

SEMILLON

Sémillon, far more than CHARDONNAY, should be Australia's great white grape yet it has remained a well kept secret that surprisingly few wine drinkers have discovered. Planted first in the humid Hunter Valley in New South Wales, it has acquired a reputation for producing very long-lived wines that appear slightly one dimensional when they're young,

but over time develop a complex palate of deep, rich, caramelised pineapple, honey and toasted nut flavours. (The most remarkable thing is that although they taste oaked many aren't.)

Sémillon has also proved a success in the Barossa and Clare Valleys in South Australia where it is made in a more openly fruity style, and in Western Australia where it is frequently blended as in Bordeaux with Sauvignon, resulting in wines with a scintillating lime and pineapple flavour. ☆☆

VIN JAUNE

A totally distinctive style of wine made in a very similar way to fino sherry. The most famous example is from the tiny appellation of **Château-Chalon** in the Jura region in France. ☆☆☆

OTHER WORLD-CLASS WHITES

There are ambitious winemakers all over the world who produce distinctive and individual white wines that don't fall into any neat pigeon-hole other than the fact that they're not CHARDONNAY – well, not pure Chardonnay at least. Examples are Aimée Guibert's **Mas de Daumas Gassac Blanc**, Randall Grahm's **Le Sophiste** (which is modelled on the great Rhône whites) and the new "white **Grange**" being developed by Australian giant Penfolds. ☆☆→☆☆☆

Storing and serving

Wines like this repay the same care as the winemaker puts into them. If you buy them young don't drink them immediately: store them on their sides in a cool, dark place. Don't chill them too much before you serve them and don't be afraid to open them an hour or so before you pour them into a generously sized wine glass. Inexpensive oaky Chardonnnays will last for a couple of years. Most New World Chardonnay is at its best three to five years old, top white burgundy from five to eight years and the very best white wines for up to 15–20 years. Australian Sémillons and Marsannes are also long-lived. They'll be fine for four to eight years.

AROMATIC AND MEDIUM-DRY WHITES

Of all the different wine styles this is by far the most eclectic, covering an extraordinary number of widely differing flavours. None of them is exactly a mainstream taste – though there are wines that have a fanatical following. Chardonnay never quite excites a Chardonnay lover the way a fine Riesling excites a Riesling devotee.

The common thread which distinguishes them from other white wines is some kind of aromatic or floral quality which makes them taste not sweet, but not quite dry either. In most cases this sweetness is offset by a crisp acidity so that the overall effect is deliciously refreshing.

Germany has most to offer in this style, but, unfortunately, has the distinction of producing some of the least exciting wine in the world as well as some of the best. Sadly, many consumers whose wine drinking experience starts with German wine never get beyond the dreariest bottles, then abandon them as unsophisticated when their wine tastes change. Alsace, another great producer of aromatic wines, and with traditionally close links to Germany, gets tarred with the same brush.

The flavour of most of the wines in this section comes from the grapes themselves. Whereas the taste of a Chardonnay often owes as much to the type of oak it is aged in as to the fruit, wines like Riesling and Gewürztraminer are made without going near a new oak barrel. Traditional producers still use big oak casks, but most are so old that they impart very little flavour of their own. The emphasis is on the vineyard rather than the winery – a question of obtaining the best possible fruit from the best possible sites, then letting it speak for itself.

Dry or sweet?

The big variation between, say, one Riesling and another, is in the level of sweetness. That depends on the grapes' ripeness when picked and how dry or sweet the winemaker intends the wine to be (see pages 26–31).

All these variations are reflected in a multiplicity of classifications. In Germany better quality dry wines are labelled "Kabinett", "Spätlese" or "Auslese", but "Auslese" and occasionally "Spätlese" can also be quite sweet. The same is true of "Vendange Tardive" (late picked) in Alsace. It isn't always easy to see what is going on in a bottle, even from the label; so don't be afraid to ask just how dry or sweet a wine is. It doesn't indicate a lack of know-how – quite the reverse!

The other common characteristic of many of these wines is just how long they can age; some of the top Rieslings and some of the Loire's best Chenin Blanc-based wines like Vouvray and Savennières will last for decades. This is not a flavour that appeals to everyone. Riesling, for example, acquires over time a distinctive kerosene flavour that is a far cry from the clean fruit flavours of most modern varietals.

It may be for this reason that the more aromatic grapes have not made huge headway among New World producers whose consumers are used to more upfront fruit flavours. But, with the constant demand for new experiences among more adventurous wine drinkers, the situation is changing. Australia is acquiring a name for its uniquely limey full-bodied Rieslings and New Zealand looks set to follow suit. And aromatic grapes like Riesling and Gewürztraminer look like a promising avenue of specialisation for the smaller wine-producing areas of North America such as British Columbia, Oregon, Ontario and New York State.

In fact, it is the image much more than the reality of many of these wines that holds people back. When they taste them they like them – and even more so when they find out how low in alcohol they are. For today's adventurous health-conscious wine drinker this light but beguilingly flavoursome style of wine has a great deal to recommend it.

Label clues

It can be difficult to tell how sweet this type of wine is but "Spätlese", "Auslese" or "Vendange Tardive" generally indicate a more concentrated wine. Look out, too, for the words "demi-sec" and "halbtrocken" which mean medium-dry. Alcohol levels are also a clue. A low alcohol content indicates a lighter, crisper style of wine. And check the vintage: older wines are more likely to have those pungent lime and kerosene flavours.

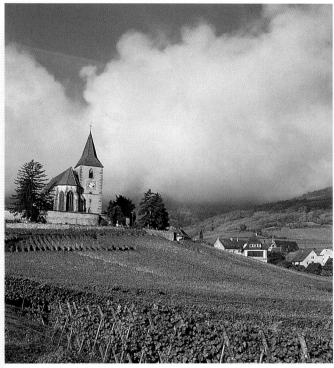

Above The picturesque village of Hunawihr in Alsace is surrounded by some of the region's finest vineyards.

Far left The spectacular steep banks of the River Mosel in Germany provide ideal conditions for ripening the Riesling grape. The vineyards are angled towards the sun which is reflected back up to the vines by the water.

Starting points	
Light/floral	**Rich/aromatic**
Sylvaner	Australian Riesling
Riesling Kabinett	Riesling Spätlese
	Tokay-Pinot Gris
Fragrant/spicy	**Medium-dry**
Torrontes	Vouvray
Dry Muscat	New World Colombard
Viognier	
Gewürztraminer	

ALBARINO

Fashionable (and consequently expensive) Spanish grape variety grown in Galicia in the north of Spain which makes appealingly delicate, aromatic whites wines with a subtle peachy flavour. It should be drunk young, but not too soon after bottling. About a year after harvest is ideal. ☆☆→☆☆☆

ANJOU & SAUMUR BLANC – demi-sec

Medium-dry versions of Anjou Blanc and Saumur Blanc from the Loire region of France are sold alongside their dry counterparts, but are rarely particularly exciting. ☆→☆☆

AUSTRALIAN "DRY WHITES"

It may seem odd to put a so-called dry white in this section, but many basic wines that are labelled "Dry White" are not strictly dry at all. This is particularly true of wines from New World countries such as Australia, New Zealand, Chile and Argentina which contain enough of an aromatic grape like MULLER-THURGAU, MUSCAT or TORRONTES to give them a slightly floral character. (Check the back label for words such as "fragrant" or "aromatic".) ☆→☆☆

CHENIN BLANC – mature, dry

Like RIESLING the top Chenin Blancs of the Loire develop a distinctive aromatic character after several years in the bottle, becoming richly honeyed with an almost nutty savouriness. Only the best wines like

dry **Vouvrays** and **Savennières** are worth keeping this long – and there isn't much of them about. ☆☆→☆☆☆

COLOMBARD

Although generally regarded as a dry white wine, Colombard is often made by Australian and South African winemakers in a slightly sweetish style which makes it a good choice for those looking for an off-dry white. CHARDONNAY that is blended with Colombard will also tend to be left with comparatively high levels of residual sugar. ☆

CONDRIEU

Expensive and highly sought-after, this northern Rhône white wine is VIOGNIER at its most exotically perfumed best. Even rarer (and more stratospheric in price) are the wines from the tiny neighbouring appellation **Château-Grillet**. ☆☆☆

FURMINT

Best-known for the part it plays in Hungary's great sweet wine Tokay (see pages 92–97), this grape is also used to make spicy, slightly earthy whites which are drier and more full-bodied than most aromatic wines. ☆→☆☆

GEWURZTRAMINER

The tasting terms that are commonly used of Gewürztraminer – rose petals, lychees and Turkish delight – underline its status as the

world's most exotic-flavoured white wine grape. It is still a wine that is primarily associated with Alsace in France where it is at its richly spicy best, but it has also attracted a fair amount of attention from New World producers. Inexpensive versions from South Africa, Chile and California tend to be fresher and more floral. Those from New Zealand, Canada and Oregon are more complex. ☆→☆☆☆

GRUNER VELTLINER – mature

Top quality Grüner Veltliner, which is grown mainly in the Wachau region of Austria, ages very much like the best RIESLING Spätlese, developing powerful aromatic spicy flavours. The best-quality wines are classified as *smaragd* and must have an alcohol content of more than 12 per cent. ☆☆→☆☆☆

HARSLEVELU

An increasingly popular Hungarian grape being used on its own or as a named component of blends with other indigenous grapes such as FURMINT to make inexpensive, crisp, aromatic whites. Low-priced Eastern European whites from Hungary, Bulgaria and Slovenia often have this kind of character – look out for the term "country wine". ☆

IRSAI OLIVER

An aromatic grape variety (also spelt Irsay Oliver) mainly planted in Hungary, Slovenia and the Czech Republic. It has a slightly MUSCAT-like flavour. ☆

LAMBRUSCO

Pallid, sweetish, slightly fizzy Italian white from Emilia-Romagna that does little justice to the original crisp, lively red wines of the same name that come from the region. Less popular than it once was. ☆

LASKI RIESLING

The name used in Slovenia for the Welschriesling grape, largely used to make dull, oversweetened whites that acquired considerable popularity during the heyday of LIEBFRAUMILCH under the brandname Lutomer Riesling. In fact, the grape can produce some deliciously fresh, aromatic whites, but they are rarely available outside the country. ☆

LIEBFRAUMILCH
and other medium-dry German whites

Cheap German semi-sweet wines such as Liebfraumilch, **Hock**, **Piesporter Michelsberg** and **Niersteiner** used to account for a large proportion of the market. But now they are increasingly (and justifiably) being eclipsed by better quality wines that offer more than simple sweetness. ☆

MULLER-THURGAU

A cross between RIESLING and SYLVANER, Müller-Thurgau has been the undistinguished mainstay of LIEBFRAUMILCH and many of Germany's cheaper whites. It is also used by English producers of medium-dry styles. But some of the crisp, clean and fruity bottles emerging from New Zealand show that the grape has more potential than has up to now been realised. ☆→☆☆

MUSCAT

Whether you regard dry Muscat as dry or not depends on your palate. Most of course is very sweet – only suitable for drinking with a dessert – but there are drier versions, particularly in Alsace and down in the Languedoc in the south of France which the locals would drink as an aperitif. The Alsace version is particularly fine – light, elegant grapey and refreshing. A small proportion of Muscat is often used by a winemaker in a blend to give his wine a more pronounced floral or aromatic character. Dry Muscats are also popular in Hungary and can offer good value for money. ☆→☆☆

RETSINA

A controversial style of Greek wine which has the distinctive aroma and flavour of pine needles (some rudely say disinfectant) which actually comes from infusing lumps of resin in the fermenting wine. It comes in both white and rosé versions and should be well-chilled. ☆

RIESLING

Germany Riesling has suffered badly from being confused with inexpensive German wines like Liebfraumilch which are made from entirely different grapes. But genuine Riesling's

Food and occasions

These idiosyncratic wines are not to everyone's taste so it's a case of knowing your guest. Most work better as an aperitif rather than a wine to take you through the meal, though there are some matches made in heaven: Australian Riesling with spicy Thai food, Gewürztraminer with the delicate flavours of Chinese cuisine, Tokay-Pinot Gris with foie gras.

unique balance of refreshingly crisp acidity and delicate sweetness makes it taste like no other wine on earth.

How then do you tell the good from the bad? The best guide is the classification system for higher quality (QmP) wines: they are labelled according to their level of ripeness. The three grades that apply to dry (as opposed to dessert wines) are Kabinett, Spätlese, and Auslese. Kabinett wines are light and crisp, Spätlese (literally, late picked) fuller and more rounded and Auslese (which is made from very ripe grapes and normally made into a sweeter style of wine) richer still. Winemakers also use the word "trocken" or "halbtrocken" (medium-dry) to indicate that their wine is made in a drier style.

There are also differences in style between one growing area and another. The Mosel-Saar-Ruwer produces Riesling at its most rarefied and racy, very low in alcohol, deliciously light. The wines from the Rheingau, and increasingly the Pfalz are richer and more full-bodied with a lush almost peachy character. The Nahe and the Rheinhessen are more varied in quality with the best of the wines from the Nahe leaning towards the style of the Mosel and those of the Rheinhessen (which is still an area that produces huge quantities of low grade wine) being more similar to those of the Rheingau and Pfalz.

The other big dividing line is between young and mature Riesling. Young Riesling, particularly that from the Mosel, can taste toothacheingly sharp but give it a few years and it develops a gloriously lush limey, almost petrolly character (which is a great deal nicer than it sounds). Others acquire a softer, richer more honeyed flavour. The best will continue to improve for several years. ☆☆→☆☆☆

Alsace These Rieslings are bigger and more alcoholic than Germany's with richer fruit flavours and a touch of spice, though again, like Germany, there are variations in quality. The most sumptuous are the Vendange Tardive (late picked) Rieslings, particularly those from the top Grand Cru vineyards. ☆☆→☆☆☆☆

Australia A good starting point for first time Riesling drinkers, Australian Rieslings share the same full-bodied fruity character as their other wines. The best come from the Clare and Eden Valleys in South Australia where they develop a marvellously tangy limey character. Where delicate German Rieslings are for sipping, these are quite wonderful with food. ☆☆→☆☆☆

New Zealand With a cooler climate than Australia, New Zealand Riesling (an increasingly popular variety in this country) is lighter and more elegant than its Antipodean counterpart with more of the ripe peachy notes and kerosene character you get in the warmer growing areas of Germany. ☆☆→☆☆☆

North America Up to now Riesling has never really taken off in the United States. In California and the Pacific Northwest where it is known as Johannisberg Riesling, it has traditionally been used to make straightforward light, citrussy, off-dry whites for everyday drinking. Some individual producers in both Oregon and Washington State are now making their Riesling in a more classic European style – closer in style to the very promising Rieslings which are emerging from Ontario and New York State. ☆☆→☆☆☆

Eastern and Central Europe Riesling is grown widely (though not very distinctively) throughout Eastern and Central Europe (some of it is the inferior Welschriesling). It is most successful in Austria's Wachau region (which produces wines of a similar style and quality to Alsace). ☆→☆☆☆

SCHEUREBE

A comparatively new grape variety (a cross between RIESLING and SILVANER) which has found favour with a number of Germany's top winemakers, particularly in the Pfalz. It can produce lovely lush, spicy whites with a seductive interplay of grapefruit and exotic fruits. ☆☆→☆☆☆

SEYVAL BLANC

A relatively undistinguished French hybrid grape popular in England and other cooler regions including Canada and New York State for making crisp, floral, as well as medium-dry whites. ☆→☆☆

SYLVANER

The lightest style of the wines from Alsace, Sylvaner produces a fresh, slightly floral wine that is markedly drier than German white in a similar price bracket. It is also one of the grapes used to make a light, fruity white called Edelzwicker – rarely found outside Alsace, but a simple, refreshing wine to drink when you are visiting the region. (The German name for the grape is Silvaner.) ☆→☆☆

TOKAY-PINOT GRIS

Confusingly, Pinot Gris is often called Tokay-Pinot Gris in Alsace, but should not be confused with Hungarian Tokay (an entirely different wine and much sweeter – *see* pages 92–97.) Alsace Pinot Gris is a much richer style than that grown elsewhere and the best examples have an exotic musky character. Vendange Tardive versions can be comparatively sweet (*see* also pages 92–97). ☆☆→☆☆☆

TORRONTES

Originally a Spanish grape variety, Torrontes has become Argentina's most successful white wine. It produces light floral, intensely perfumed whites which make for charmingly easy drinking when young but which fade very quickly after a year or so. Be sure to drink the current vintage. ☆

VIOGNIER

This has become something of a cult grape variety. For years it languished in obscurity in the Rhône Valley where only insiders knew it was the grape from which the great aromatic white CONDRIEU was made (*see* above). Now it's planted all over southern France and is increasingly popular in California. It is a frustratingly tricky grape variety to handle. Purists complain that it seldom reaches the heights it does in the Rhône, but most wine drinkers would be more than satisfied with the pretty aromatic apricot and peach-flavoured wines that are now made at a much more modest price. ☆☆→☆☆☆

VOUVRAY – demi-sec

The most highly regarded medium-dry white is demi-sec Vouvray which comes from the Loire region of France. While some can be as dull as other less distinguished medium-dry Loire whites, the best wines from individual producers such as Brédif and Huët have a deliciously rich, smooth honeyed flavour. A similar style is available from the **Montlouis** appellation, the other side of Loire. NB Make sure you look carefully at the label. Both are also made in dry (sec) and sweet (moelleux) versions. ☆☆→☆☆☆

WHITE ZINFANDEL

Confusingly the hugely popular White Zin is not really a white wine at all as it is made from the red Zinfandel grape. The same applies to **White Grenache** and **White Merlot**. (*See* Rosé section pages 82–85.) ☆

Storing and serving

This type of wine benefits from being well chilled. While light fragrant varieties such as Sylvaner, Torrontes and Viognier should be drunk soon after you buy them, others like Chenin Blanc, Grüner Veltliner, Riesling and Tokay-Pinot Gris can last for many years. By and large it is the richer, more concentrated (and inevitably the more expensive) wines which last the longest. See also individual listings.

LIGHT, FRUITY REDS

People are attracted to lighter red wines for a variety of reasons. Firstly it's a good starting point for the new red wine drinker, not only from the point of view of their palate (these wines are neither tough or tannic), but their pocket. Almost all inexpensive reds come into this category, whether it's a *vin rouge*, *vino rosso* or *vino tinto*. They're the kind of wines you find served by the carafe at a French café or an Italian *trattoria*.

By contrast, this style also appeals to experienced wine drinkers who gear their wine choice to the occasion and the time of year. For them lesser-known Loire reds or a delicate Pinot Noir make perfect summer drinking or an interestingly unconventional choice with fish.

Finally, there are people who discover this style and stick with it. Those who prefer their red wine soft and fruity, rather than full-bodied and oaky, who enjoy the sheer refreshing gulpability of a Valpolicella and a Beaujolais. Truly this style has something for everyone.

Most wines are light because they are designed to be so, usually because the producer has to make them to a price. The traditional way, much favoured by small winegrowers all over Europe, was to allow your vines to produce as prolifically as possible and to do as little as you could get away with to the resulting wine. The result was often dull and dilute.

Hi-tech winemaking

These days when quality is at a premium, wines owe their style far more to what goes on in the winery. Producing a light red wine involves sophisticated techniques like carbonic maceration (*see* pages 26–31) to preserve its bright fruit flavours, fermenting it at cool temperatures in stainless steel and avoiding the use of expensive oak barrels which not only push up the price, but make the wine fuller-bodied.

This is why grapes like Grenache and Tempranillo, better-known for big-tasting wines, are in this section. The difference is in the degree of concentration. Where a winemaker uses grapes from younger vines, or less favoured vineyards the wine will be lighter – as low as 11 per cent.

Climate also has a part to play in how a red wine tastes. On the whole this is not a style of wine you generally find in the New World. In hotter climates grapes ripen more fully and that sweetness converts to higher levels of alcohol. The only New World wines you'll consistently find in this style are basic reds like a "Cape red", "Chilean red" or "California red" which are made to a price and to satisfy the maximum number of different palates. A good vintage will also make a difference, particularly in Europe. If you regularly taste Beaujolais Nouveau when it comes out, for example, you'll notice that some years it tastes much riper and fruitier than others. A simple Côtes du Rhône, too, will taste much richer and fuller in a good year like 1995 than a poor year like 1992.

There are also grapes which are naturally light and fruity and particularly attractive unoaked. This is true of both Gamay and Pinot Noir and also of the lesser-known Italian grapes that make such wines as Valpolicella. Keeping them away from oak is not only a question of keeping the cost down, but of preserving the pure flavour of the fruit. With more expensive reds such as those from the Loire, producers may age their wines in oak, but the long ripening period in that cool region gives the wines an intensity of fruit that offsets any overt oakiness.

The major variations within this style are between sharpness and smoothness. Some wines, particularly the lighter Italian wines, like Bardolino or Valpolicella, and Beaujolais, have naturally tart fruit. This can be disguised by adding sugar (chaptalisation); but better winemakers won't do this. They can be tremendously refreshing – particularly chilled during the summer, but some wine drinkers can find them uncomfortably sharp and acidic. Other grape varieties like Merlot, Pinot Noir and Dornfelder are much softer and smoother and therefore much more approachable.

What most of these wines have in common is that they offer simple, straightforward drinking. Buy them, take them home and drink them within a week, if not the same night – these are not wines to store or worry about cellaring. There is a place for them in everyone's collection.

Label clues

The two best indications of a lighter style of wine are alcohol content and vintage. Red wines under 12 degrees will almost always be light and fruity. Look out for the most recent vintage – wines that are two or three years old may start to taste fat and flabby rather than vibrantly fruity.

Above *Valpolicella in northeast Italy is the source of a large range of light red wines. The picture shows part of the "Classico" zone which, in theory offers better quality.*

Far left *The beautiful region of Beaujolais in France produces distinctively juicy, fruity light red wines.*

Starting points	
Fresh, fruity	**Soft/smooth**
Beaujolais	Italian or Hungarian Merlot
Basic burgundy	Dornfelder
Bardolino	Chilean Pinot Noir
Valpolicella	

BARBERA

 A grape responsible for a wide range of styles, some of which are quite full-bodied. The lightest is **Barbera d'Asti** from Piedmont in northwest Italy which has a tart but refreshing sour cherry flavour. ☆☆→☆☆☆

BARDOLINO

 An appealing light, fresh fruity red from the Veneto in the northeast of Italy . Very similar in style although rather less commercial than VALPOLICELLA: it tends to be lighter and often tastes less sweet. ☆→☆☆

BEAUJOLAIS

 The epitome of light fruity drinking. Made from the GAMAY grape to the south of BURGUNDY, at one stage Beaujolais's youthful cherry-flavoured style was almost unique but competition from more reliably fruity New World wines has caused its popularity to wane. Most people's first encounter with Beaujolais is **Beaujolais Nouveau**, the first wine of the vintage, released in November within a few weeks of the harvest. Except in a particularly good year it tends to be very light with a slightly confected flavour irreverently compared to bananas and bubblegum. Basic Beaujolais is often little different although wines from better producers such as Carron and Sarrau can be very fine indeed. **Beaujolais Villages**, which comes from individual villages in the region, is in theory better still (but that isn't invariably the case). Far more serious are the top ranking so-called "Cru" Beaujolais though these fall in the next section. ☆→☆☆

BLAUER ZWEIGELT

 Also known as Zweigelt, this is a popular Austrian grape variety making smooth, soft plummy reds, often at a modest price. ☆→☆☆

BLAUFRANKISCH/KEKFRANKOS

 Another indigenous Austrian grape. Unoaked it makes attractively tart berry-flavoured reds (the style usually made in Hungary where it is called Kékfrankos) but which have a nice spicy kick to them. When oaked it is richer and fuller-bodied. ☆☆→☆☆☆

BURGUNDY – inexpensive, unoaked

 Because it is generally so expensive, burgundy has the image of being a heavyweight wine. But, in fact, PINOT NOIR – the grape from which it is made – is a naturally light, fragrant variety which, when left unoaked, produces wines with a pure, intense raspberry flavour and deliciously soft, supple texture.

Most basic burgundy is simply labelled "**Bourgogne Rouge**", though producers now occasionally add the words "Pinot Noir". As in neighbouring BEAUJOLAIS, quality varies but the overall standard has improved considerably in recent years. Wines made by individual growers – often just down the road from some of the region's greatest vineyards can be very fine indeed. **Bourgogne Passe-Tout-Grains** is confusingly not really true burgundy at all but a blend of Pinot Noir and GAMAY. As you might expect from the grape varieties, it falls somewhere in style between a burgundy and Beaujolais.

Some burgundies from individual villages could also be classed as light and fruity – the most likely candidates are **Chorey-lès-Beaune**, **Marsannay**, **Monthelie**, **Rully** and occasionally **St-Aubin**. ☆☆

CABERNET FRANC – Old World

 The third element of the classic Bordeaux blend, Cabernet Franc is also used in other European wine regions, such as the LOIRE, Eastern Europe and northern Italy, to make wine on its own. Suited to cooler climates, it is capable of producing quite richly flavoured wines, but with a dryness and slight stalkiness about them that makes them taste comparatively light. Italian versions, mostly from the Friuli region in the northeast, are particularly fruity. ☆☆→☆☆☆

CINSAULT – South African

 Cinsault (also spelt Cinsaut) is widely planted in South Africa where it is used in most of its inexpensive reds – sometimes anonymously as a "**Cape Red**", sometimes in a blend with another varietal such as Pinotage, Ruby Cabernet and even Zinfandel. It has a fairly sweet, simple taste, though cheaper versions can develop a less appealing, rather rubbery flavour. ☆→☆☆

COTES DU RHONE

 Like BEAUJOLAIS, Côtes du Rhône varies considerably in quality from one producer to another and between vintages. In a warm year like 1995, or from a top Rhône producer like

Guigal, it can taste sumptuously rich and alcoholic; in a poor vintage or from a less quality conscious co-op it can be pretty weedy (Côtes du Rhône is based on GRENACHE which can taste thin if it is allowed to crop too heavily). However, standards have improved and more and more wines are soft and appealing with an attractive sweet strawberry flavour – offering the typical warmth of a southern French red without the weight that often goes with it. ☆→☆☆

DAO and young, Portuguese reds

Portuguese reds used invariably to be heavy and oaky. Not any more. Even wines like Dão these days are made in a much more upfront fruity style. (The way to tell which is which is to check the vintage. If the wine is more than two years old it's likely to have been made in the traditional style.) Most of these lighter, fruitier reds (though with Portugal you're always talking about a fuller-bodied wine than you would find, for example, in Italy) come from the up and coming areas in the centre and south of the country: the Alentejo, Estremadura and Ribatejo. Most come from co-ops but several show the influence of overseas, often Antipodean, winemakers. ☆→☆☆

DOLCETTO

This grape is grown in Piedmont in northwest Italy but makes a very different style of wine to BARBERA, characterised by its intensely vivid brambly fruit (Dolcetto means "little sweet one"). For an Italian wine it has comparatively low acidity. ☆☆

DOLE

Switzerland's most distinctive red, which comes from the Valais region in the French speaking part of the country, is a softly fruity but elegant wine. It is made predominantly from PINOT NOIR blended with a varying amount of GAMAY. ☆☆→☆☆☆

DORNFELDER – unoaked

An indigenous German grape variety which makes the country's best-known red wine. Young, unoaked versions which are smooth and softly plummy make particularly easy, approachable drinking for first-time red wine drinkers. Oaked versions are more full-bodied and substantial. ☆→☆☆

GAMAY

Although this grape variety is overwhelmingly identified with BEAUJOLAIS, it is also grown elsewhere in France, mainly in BURGUNDY and the LOIRE. (**Gamay de Touraine** is often better value than basic Beaujolais.)

In Burgundy and Switzerland it is often blended with PINOT NOIR – both red Mâcon and **Bourgogne Passe-Tout-Grains** are blends. ☆→☆☆

GRENACHE – France

This is one of those grape varieties that can be made into very different styles of wine. If Grenache is allowed to produce prolific amounts of grapes it makes light strawberry flavoured wines like COTES DU RHONE. If yields

Food and occasions

Light, fruity reds make ideal wines for all kinds of summer drinking, such as picnics and barbecues. They're good all year round for parties and for informal meals particularly with simple supper dishes like pasta and pizza.

are restricted or the resulting wine is oaked it can be a real bruiser. Price is the best guide. Cheap Grenache is likely to be light (though even then it can be surprisingly alcoholic). Moderately priced or expensive Grenache is much fuller-bodied. ☆→☆☆

LAMBRUSCO

Real red Lambrusco is worlds away from the sweet, tasteless white variety that most people identify with this wine. Hovering between still and sparkling, it is exuberantly fruity with a tart red berry flavour.

It's well worth looking in specialist Italian delicatessens for the more traditional style of Lambrusco rather than the sweeter more commercial versions you find in supermarkets. ☆

LOIRE

The Loire Valley is Europe's most northerly red wine producing area which gives its reds a particularly distinctive character. Broadly they're characterised by a purity of fruit and a marked lack of sweetness that means that even in a good vintage they taste comparatively light. Among the wines made from CABERNET FRANC there is often a herbaceous note, a hint of green pepper and a curious slatiness that gives them a slightly austere, astringent quality. But it's always accompanied by a lightness and elegance that makes them particularly beguiling. (Unfortunately the fervent following they have gained among wine lovers – particularly Parisian ones – has resulted in high prices but, unlike other classic French wines, they rarely disappoint.)

The three best-known wines are **Bourgueil**, **Chinon** and **Saumur-Champigny** which are all based on Cabernet Franc. Chinon tends to be the softest, and fruitiest of the three; Bourgueil and Saumur-Champigny have the greater ageing capacity (up to 10 years from the best producers).

The other major Loire red is **Sancerre Rouge**, much less well-known than its white counterpart, a delicate, silky strawberry-flavoured wine which is made from PINOT NOIR. Red wines are also made from GAMAY in **Touraine** and **St-Pourcain** in central France. Less well-known appellations are **Anjou-Villages** and **Anjou Rouge**, **Menetou-Salon** and **Saumur Rouge**. ☆☆→☆☆☆

MERLOT – unoaked

Normally associated with a much richer, fuller style of wine, inexpensive European Merlot can be quite light-bodied. That is particularly the case in northern Italy where light, fruity quaffing wines such as **Merlot del Veneto** are sometimes as low as 11.5 degrees. Cheap Merlots from Hungary and from the **Languedoc** (usually marketed as **Vin de Pays d'Oc**) also offer simple fruity drinking. ☆→☆☆

MONTEPULCIANO D'ABRUZZO

A smoothly fruity, quaffing wine from central Italy. The cheapest bottles can be rather weak and weedy but be prepared to pay a little more and you should get a wine that's attractively juicy and supple. These wines are generally a reliable choice in restaurants, offering better value than **Chianti**. ☆→☆☆

PINOT NOIR – unoaked

With BURGUNDY still the benchmark for most Pinot Noir producers, the unoaked wines you find outside the region are mainly made in the same forward, fruity style. Burgundy lovers are likely to find greatest satisfaction from California and Oregon in the US which have succeeded better than anywhere else in replicating that unique combination of soft, raspberry fruit and fine, delicate acidity. Chile's Pinot Noir is slightly softer.

Lighter styles of Pinot Noir can also be found in Switzerland, Austria and Germany (where it is known as **Spätburgunder**), though producers tend to justify the high prices it fetches in these countries by making it in a more full-bodied style. ☆☆→☆☆☆

PROVENCE & THE RHONE

There is a whole host of other appellations in the Rhône and across southern France which offer a similar style of light, fruity drinking: **Coteaux d'Aix en Provence**, **Côtes du Lubéron**, **Coteaux du Tricastin** and **Côtes du Ventoux** are on the Rhône/Provence side. The rapidly improving **Côtes du Roussillon** is closer to the Spanish border. ☆☆→☆☆☆

SANGIOVESE – Italian

As the mainstay of **Chianti** (see next section), Sangiovese usually counts as a medium-bodied, if not a heavyweight wine but where it has been released as a varietal, for example as **Sangiovese di Romana** or **Sangiovese di Toscana**, it's more often just a simple light, quaffable red. ☆→☆☆

SARDINIA & SICILY

 As reliable sources of bargain basement drinking, most of the wines of Sardinia and Sicily are produced in this style. Sardinia has its own grape variety, the **Monica di Sardegna**, which makes simple fruity reds. Sicily's vast output is improving, thanks, in part, to input from flying winemakers. But given its hot climate, the likelihood is that as quality improves, the reds will become more concentrated and full-bodied. ☆→☆☆

SPANNA

 The Nebbiolo grape by another name, Spanna, which comes from the northeast of Piedmont, has a similar robust, brambly style to DOLCETTO. ☆→☆☆

TARRANGO

 A recently introduced Australian grape variety which makes vividly fruity, soft sweetish reds – very similar in style to a BEAUJOLAIS. Almost all of it is produced by Brown Brothers of Victoria. ☆☆

TEMPRANILLO – young, unoaked

 Young Tempranillo, known as **Tempranillo Joven** in **Rioja** and **Navarra** is a far cry from the sweetly pruney wines that emerge after months of oak-ageing. Even so it can be quite big and robust and only just falls into this category on the grounds of the sheer vivacity of its fruit. In **La Mancha** and **Valdepeñas** the same grape is known as Cencibel. ☆→☆☆

TEROLDEGO ROTALIANO

 A soft, smooth red produced in the Trentino region of northeast Italy. Rather more like a Swiss or Austrian than an Italian red with intense fruit and less marked acidity. ☆

VALPOLICELLA

 Gross commercialisation has disguised the fact that Valpolicella can be a really delightful wine: full and generous with a distinctive ripe cherry flavour. In theory at least, wines labelled "Classico" should be of better quality. "Superiore" means they must contain at least 12 degrees. Look for wines from individual producers such as Bertani, Masi and Tedeschi. ☆→☆☆

VIN DE PAYS

 The description "vin de pays" on a label doesn't necessarily mean the wine inside the bottle is light and fruity, but given that most of these wines are relatively inexpensive, there's a fairly good chance that it will be. The main exception are the **Vins de Pays d'Oc**. Most of these are made from a single grape variety and in a full-bodied New World style. ☆→☆☆

VINI DA TAVOLA

 Most inexpensive Italian reds, often simply described as a "vino da tavola", are light and fruity with a characteristic crisp (and occasionally sharp) acidity. The majority come from the north of the country – particularly from the Veneto. ☆→☆☆

Storing and serving

This is one style of wine that's not really worth keeping for long – more expensive burgundies and Loire reds excepted. Don't be afraid to serve these wines lightly chilled, particularly in the summer.

SMOOTH, MEDIUM-BODIED REDS

Smooth might seem an odd word to use about wine. But the experience of drinking wine is as much about its feel in your mouth as the flavour itself. Many people prefer a wine, particularly a red wine, that is neither too acidic and sharp, as is often the case with lighter wines, or wines that are too strong and alcoholic. This is why this style of wine is so popular.

It includes all the world's best-known wines, from the great French classics of Bordeaux and Burgundy, to the exuberantly fruity reds of Australia and Chile. The big divide is between wines made in a more traditional, Old World style and those with the more overtly fruity character of the New World.

If you take a grape like Cabernet Sauvignon, for example, in Bordeaux it will make an essentially dry wine, fruity certainly, but not as full and definitely not as sweet as a Cabernet from Chile or South Africa. That is mainly due to the climate but also due to the techniques New World winemakers use to accentuate the fruit flavours of their wines.

How you respond to these contrasting styles depends very much on how long you've been drinking wine and what your starting point is. If the first red wine you drank was Bordeaux and you've been drinking it for 20 years, you may well find a Chilean Cabernet Sauvignon too sweet for your palate. But if you only recently started drinking red wine you would probably find the Chilean Cabernet much more acceptable and a classic Bordeaux too austere. Bordeaux rarely has the instant appeal of New World wines. You wouldn't want to drink it on its own, but it can be far more subtle and satisfying with food.

Old World uncertainties

The challenge with the traditional wine-producing areas is finding wines that are genuinely good value. Whereas you can almost guarantee when you buy an inexpensive Australian wine that it will taste like the last bottle you bought, that's far from the case with Bordeaux and Burgundy. The combination of uncertain weather conditions which lead to marked variations in vintage and the fact that the best-known wines are often over-priced means that it's difficult to predict exactly what you're going to get. The best tip is to take advice from a specialist wine shop or a knowledgeable sommelier, but if that isn't possible, follow the guidelines under the entries for each of these regions.

Having said all this, the divisions between the Old World and the New are becoming a lot less clear cut. Although Burgundy, in the main, remains staunchly traditional, regions like Bordeaux, Chianti and Rioja are all responding to the increasing demand for more approachable wines. In Tuscany, for example, winemakers are adding small amounts of Cabernet to the traditional Sangiovese grape, while those in Spain are increasingly abandoning their old oak casks in favour of new oak barrels. Although this gives rise to criticism that all wines are beginning to taste the same, it's good news for wine drinkers who may want to widen their choice from the simple varietals of the New World, but are not yet ready to move on to the more singular tastes of well aged wine.

As with most wines what you get out of this style of wine depends very much on what you are prepared to pay. At the cheaper end of the spectrum, including wines from Eastern Europe, the Languedoc and more inexpensive wines from Australia, Chile and South Africa, the best value is to be found in varietal wines like Cabernet and Merlot with simple fruit flavours that are ready to drink straight away. If you are prepared to pay more for the wines of, say Bordeaux and Burgundy, you can reasonably expect more complex wines that are capable of maturing over time (though you may still want to drink them within months rather than years). But if you don't like full-bodied reds, avoid those that make a feature of the fact that they have been aged in oak.

Although this is not the red wine style in which you will find more unusual flavours, if you like to experiment, look out for the lesser-known appellations of big wine areas like Bordeaux, Burgundy and the Rhône, for the Beaujolais Crus, for more obscure Spanish and Italian reds and in the New World for lesser-known grapes such as Malbec and Mataro.

Label Clues

The best indication of whether a red is medium- or full-bodied is the alcohol level. Look out for wines with alcohol levels between 12 and 13 degrees. Younger vintages generally make lighter drinking. Watch out for the words "Reserve" or "Reserva" which will tend to indicate a fuller-bodied wine.

Above The Médoc region of Bordeaux produces some of the world's most sought-after wines – dry and spicy, with a subtle blackcurrant fruitiness.

Far left South African Cabernet Sauvignon generally has a lighter, leaner, less full-bodied character than may of its New World counterparts.

Starting points	
Smooth and dry	**Sweeter and fruity**
Bordeaux	Australian Shiraz blends
Chianti Classico	South African Cabernet
Rioja Crianza	Chilean Merlot

BEAUJOLAIS – Cru

Although most Beaujolais is light and fruity, the wines named after 10 particular districts or villages, the "Crus" (or growths) are generally fuller-bodied. These are **Brouilly**, **Côte de Brouilly**, **Chénas**, **Chiroubles**, **Fleurie**, **Juliénas**, **Morgon**, **Moulin à Vent**, **Régnié** and **St-Amour**. Wines vary from one producer to another, but Chiroubles, Fleurie and St-Amour are generally lighter, Morgon and Moulin à Vent more intense. ☆☆→☆☆☆

BERGERAC & other Bordeaux-style wines

Very similar wines to BORDEAUX, made from the same grape varieties, are produced in the surrounding areas. Bergerac, **Côtes de Duras**, **Côtes du Frontonnais** and **Côtes du Marmandais** are on a par with basic Bordeaux; CABERNET-dominated **Buzet** tends to be fuller-bodied. The Languedoc also produces wines in this style – particularly in **Cabardès** and **Côtes de la Malepère**. ☆→☆☆

BORDEAUX

Bordeaux is a huge wine area, producing more than Australia and five times as much as BURGUNDY. We tend to think of it in terms of its most famous and illustrious châteaux, but the vast majority of bottles it produces are classified as basic Bordeaux.

The classic Bordeaux grape varieties are CABERNET SAUVIGNON and MERLOT, with occasionally some Cabernet Franc, MALBEC or Petit Verdot. The two major grapes are perfect partners, the softer Merlot fleshing out the austere, more tannic Cabernet. But in practice, with the increasing demand for soft fruity wines, it is Merlot that increasingly dominates.

There have also been changes in wine-making. A lot of Bordeaux used to be left to macerate for days and was then aged for months in old oak casks. This meant that even young wines could be impenetrably tough and tannic. Now the emphasis is on accentuating Bordeaux's natural fruitiness, supplemented by new oak so that even the biggest wines tend to be drinkable straight away.

Even then, there is always a dryness and spiciness about Bordeaux compared to the much sweeter flavour of a New World Cabernet or Merlot – a sensation of lightness despite the fact that the flavour is full. This is particularly the case with wines with a high proportion of Cabernet.

The two things that help you pin down the style of Bordeaux is what part of the region it is from and from what kind of property. All labels indicate the area the wine comes from: the more specific that area is, the more complex the wine is likely to be. ☆→☆☆☆

BORDEAUX AC

Basic Bordeaux – or claret – can come from anywhere in the region and may have been blended from more than one area. Most is simple, young, fruity and inexpensive. **Bordeaux Supérieur** on the label means simply that it contains more alcohol. ☆→☆☆

BURGUNDY

With so many different names, so many different producers, Burgundy is maddeningly difficult to pin down, but what distinguishes its wines is a generous sweetness and softness that belies its often high levels of alcohol. This is without doubt PINOT NOIR at its finest, with an intoxicating purity of flavour, sensuously silky texture, and occasionally a high octane blast of supercharged fruit and spice.

The best starting point is the formal classification system. The two categories that fall into this section are "village wines" (named after the village in which they are produced) and Premiers Crus – better quality village wines to which the name of the vineyard is attached, eg Savigny-lès-Beaune-Les Serpentières. Premiers Crus tend to be more full-bodied and have greater ageing capacity.

Lighter styles include all the "Côtes" and "Villages" – wines which don't carry specific village names, but which may be of decent quality. They include **Bourgogne** CÔTE CHALONNAISE, **Hautes-Côtes de Nuits**, CÔTE DE NUITS-**Villages**, **Hautes-Côtes de Beaune** and CÔTE DE BEAUNE-**Villages**.

Village wines are the next step up. People tend to be impressed by the best-known names such as **Gevrey-Chambertin** in the CÔTE DE NUITS but the vineyards of a less famous appellation which may literally be just down the road can offer far better value. The highest classification of Grand Cru for wines which come from the region's best vineyards tend to be fuller-bodied and/or rare (*see* pages 72–77 and 78–81).

All these generalisations, of course, can be affected by the vintage. Burgundy is susceptible to bad weather and the grapes don't always ripen fully. A burgundy from an indifferent year like 1994 will generally be less full-bodied than one in a good vintage like 1995 – though a top producer will still make a better wine in a bad year than a poor producer will in a good one. ☆☆→☆☆☆

CABERNET SAUVIGNON

In warmer climates than those of BORDEAUX and southwest France, Cabernet Sauvignon tends to be much richer and riper, but there are some examples of less heavy wines. These include less expensive Cabernets from Italy, the Languedoc and South Africa and most young Bulgarian Cabernets – though these are often untypically sweet and fruity. ☆→☆☆☆

CHIANTI

One of Italy's best-known wines, made in Tuscany from the Sangiovese grape. Like many of the world's most famous wines, the quality of Chianti varies hugely, but most combine rich, plummy fruit with a typically (for Italian wines) high acidity. Within a couple of years more traditionally made versions develop a sweet, slightly, raisiny pruney flavour. But, like everywhere else in the wine world, Tuscany is changing and Chianti is increasingly made in a more obviously fruity style, usually by adding a small amount (up to 10 per cent) of CABERNET SAUVIGNON, MERLOT or SYRAH to the wine instead of the traditional proportion of white grape varieties. Better quality Chianti comes from one of seven subregions, the best-known of which are **Classico** and **Rufina**. ☆→☆☆☆

COTE DE BEAUNE

Although better-known for its whites, this, the southern half of BURGUNDY's Côte d'Or – also produces significant reds including **Aloxe-Corton**, **Pommard** and **Volnay**, though, in general, the wines are lighter and more supple than those of the COTE DE NUITS. For value try **Auxey-Duresses**, **Monthelie**, **Pernand-Vergelesses**, **Santenay**, **Savigny-lès-Beaune** and **St-Aubin**. ☆☆

COTE CHALONNAISE

BURGUNDY wine region just to the south of the COTE DE BEAUNE producing wines that offer comparatively good value for the region. Look out for **Givry**, **Mercurey** and **Rully** (particularly on restaurant wine lists). ☆☆

COTE DE NUITS

The part of the Côte d'Or where most top red BURGUNDIES are produced. Some, like **Nuits-St-Georges** and **Gevrey-Chambertin**, are (or should be) more full-bodied and fall into the next section. Others, like **Chambolle-Musigny** and **Vosne-Romanée**, are lighter, lusher and more supple. **Fixin** and **Marsannay** offer some of the best value in the region. ☆☆→☆☆☆

COTES DU RHONE-VILLAGES

Full and fruity, these are generally much more substantial than basic Côtes du Rhône. If the village name, such as **Cairanne** or **Valréas**, is given on the label, the quality is likely to be higher still. ☆☆

CROZES-HERMITAGE
– and other lighter Rhône reds

Some of the less expensive Rhône appellations such as Crozes-Hermitage, **Gigondas**, **Lirac** and **Vacquéyras** are also capable of

Food and occasions

The occasion and your choice of guests are likely to be the most important factors determining your choice of wine. More traditional wines like Bordeaux, burgundy and Rioja are better for more formal occasions and older guests; modern varietals like Cabernet and Merlot tend to be better for informal parties and a younger age group. The same division extends to food. Old World wines suit the more classic cuisines of France and Italy – New World wines, more spicy, adventurous flavours.

producing generously fruity reds, but without the weight of a **Cornas** or a **Châteauneuf-du-Pape**. Another name to look out for is **Costières de Nîmes**, technically in the Languedoc, but making vigorously fruity, brambly reds similar to those of the Rhône. ☆☆

CRUS BOURGEOIS

An official ranking of châteaux in the MEDOC which, while in theory less prestigious than the **Crus Classés** (the first five growths – *see* page 80) generally offers the winedrinker much better value for money. Good examples include Châteaux d'Angludet, Chasse-Spleen, Haut-Marbuzet, Meyney, Montbrison, de Pez, Phélan-Ségur, Potensac and Poujeaux. Other Bordeaux to look out for are those referred to as **Petits Châteaux** – wines that miss out on the official classification system but can offer solid, reliable drinking. ☆☆→☆☆☆

FRONSAC

A good example of a Bordeaux appellation that (along with neighbouring **Canon-Fronsac**) offers better value than some of the household names. Just next door to ST-EMILION, its wines share the same soft, fruity character. Other underrated appellations on the "right bank" include **Côtes de Castillon**, **Côtes de Francs** and **Côtes de Bourg**. ☆☆

HAUT-MEDOC

A region made famous by it four most famous communes – **Margaux**, **St-Julien**, **Pauillac** and **St-Estèphe** which contain most of

---

BORDEAUX's finest châteaux (the CRUS CLASSES). Less well-known are the communes of **Moulis** and **Listrac** which are frequently the source of excellent wines, but at less elevated prices. ☆☆→☆☆☆☆

MEDOC & GRAVES

The two BORDEAUX appellations that sandwich the more prestigious HAUT-MEDOC on the left bank of the Gironde make a slightly lighter, fruitier style of Bordeaux. These days MERLOT tends to dominate, rather than the more traditional CABERNET SAUVIGNON. ☆☆→☆☆☆☆

MALBEC – Argentina and Chile

This variety is particularly successful in the Mendoza region of Argentina, producing soft, fleshy reds with ripe, smooth plummy fruit. A similar style of wine is made in Chile. More elegant wines can be produced by blending with CABERNET SAUVIGNON or MERLOT. ☆

MERLOT

There's a fundamental sweetness and generosity about Merlot that ensures that even the most concentrated expensively oaked wines are smoothly enjoyable. The most elegant examples undoubtedly come from BORDEAUX, but serious wines are also to be found in Chile, South Africa and above all, California where "Merlot mania" has reached epidemic proportions. By and large, the more inexpensive bottles tend to be softer and sweeter than wines which are bolstered by oak. If you prefer a lighter style, try

---

inexpensive Merlot from the Languedoc, South Africa or Bulgaria (but take care with Bulgarian wines that it's from a recent vintage), Chile has the most lushly fruity Merlots, California the most concentrated. ☆→☆☆

MOURVEDRE/MATARO

This grape variety has an aromatic, slightly perfumed quality which isn't immediately obvious in such full-bodied wines as **Bandol** (or in Spain where it is called Monastrell), but which plays a significant part in many southern French reds such as **Faugères**. As Mataro, the name normally used in Australia, it mainly produces simple juicy fruity reds. ☆☆→☆☆☆

NAVARRA – and modern Spanish reds

Like all other wine-producing countries, Spain is responding to world-wide demand for easy drinking reds. That is particularly the case in its most go-ahead wine-producing regions, Navarra, **Costers del Segre**, **Penedès**, **Somontano** and the **Terra Alta**, many of which are growing non-traditional grape varieties like CABERNET SAUVIGNON and MERLOT. Also worth looking out for are the new **Vinos de la Tierra** (the Spanish equivalent of French *vin de pays*). ☆→☆☆

PINOT NOIR – New World, oaked

The majority of high-quality New World Pinot Noir falls into this category, even when it is labelled "Reserve". That includes most Pinots from California and Oregon, from New Zealand and from newcomers Canada and

New York State. Australian Pinot Noir can be much more heavy and concentrated, though there are individual producers like Coldstream Hills and Mountadam who aim for a more BURGUNDIAN style. ☆☆→☆☆☆

RIOJA – modern style

Although Rioja is generally identified with a more mature style of wine (*see* pages 78–81) increasingly producers are ignoring the traditional classification of Reserva and Gran Reserva, which necessitates the wines spending several years in oak, and producing their wines in a more youthful, fruity style. Apart from the vintage, clues to look out for on a label are the words **Joven** (young) or **Tempranillo** (the main grape variety used in Rioja) which do not normally appear on more traditional wines. The description **Crianza** which states the wine has spent 12 months in wood (increasingly new oak barrels rather than the traditional casks) indicates an oakier, more full-bodied style. ☆☆

ROSSO DI MONTALCINO – and other Italian reds

Two good alternatives to more expensive Tuscan reds are Rosso di Montalcino and **Rosso di Montepulciano** – less grand versions of **Brunello di Montalcino** and **Vino Nobile di Montepulciano** respectively. From the Marches, **Rosso Conero** and **Rosso Piceno** both offer good value while some of the better quality wines among the northern Italian reds mentioned in the last section, such as **Barbera** and **Valpolicella**, can also make relatively robust drinking. ☆☆

RUBY CABERNET

A cross of CABERNET SAUVIGNON and Carignan producing far from subtle, but richly fruity reds. It often acts as a useful blending partner for cheaper wines in the New World, especially in California, South Africa and, to a lesser extent, Australia. ☆

ST-EMILION & POMEROL

Two BORDEAUX appellations producing some of the region's most lush, supple wines (including **Pétrus** and **Le Pin**). Unlike the MEDOC, better wines are designated Grand Cru Classé and Premier Grand Cru Classé (the former offer better value). Bargains can also be found in "satellite" villages such as **Montagne-St-Emilion** and **Lussac-St-Emilion**. ☆☆→☆☆☆

SHIRAZ BLENDS – Australia

Although Shiraz on its own makes a robust, full-bodied wine, it is frequently blended with lighter grape varieties such as CABERNET SAUVIGNON, Grenache and RUBY CABERNET to make smoother, more approachable reds. ☆

SYRAH – France

The mainstay of many big southern French reds, particularly those from the Rhône, when Syrah appears on its own on the label, for example, as a **Vin de Pays d'Oc**, it tends to be made in a lighter style. But still expect that characteristic mix of vivid red berry fruit and peppery spice. ☆

Storing and serving

The less-expensive wines in this style are designed to be drunk relatively quickly, usually within the year. More expensive wines will last a good deal longer, though if you want to avoid them beginning to taste like a well matured wine, you would do best to drink them within a couple of years. Bigger, more expensive wines also repay opening an hour before serving, unlike cheaper wines which can be poured straight away.

FULL-BODIED REDS

Wine drinkers rarely start off liking full-bodied reds, but there are few dedicated wine enthusiasts who don't end up loving them. This after all is as winey as wine gets: intense, concentrated and richly satisfying.

No one part of the world has a monopoly of this style of wine, though it's easier to make in a hot climate where grapes ripen more reliably than in a cooler one. Certain grape varieties also lend themselves more to fuller-bodied wines. Cabernet Sauvignon, for example, with its small, thick skinned grapes, is capable of making deeply coloured wines with a high level of tannin. The same is true of Nebbiolo, the intensely tannic grape used for the great Italian wines Barolo and Barbaresco, and of many of the Portuguese varieties like Touriga Nacional, Touriga Francesca and Tinta Barocca which are also used for making port.

But as important as either of these factors is how the resulting wine is made. Syrah, for example, will produce a much lighter wine if the vines are allowed to grow as many grapes as possible and only makes the big spicy wines associated with the variety when yields are kept right down.

Ripe, concentrated wines

To produce a deeply flavoured wine involves growing grapes on difficult sites where they don't have much access to nourishment or moisture, selecting the best bunches and picking them at the optimum moment of ripeness. It means taking grapes from older, less productive vines rather than younger, more prolific ones.

Such wines also need careful handling in the winery – leaving the juice in contact with the skins for as long as possible and fermenting at higher than average temperatures to extract maximum colour and flavour. The resulting wine is then aged in good quality oak to give it extra structure and longevity. All this helps to explain why many full-bodied wines are so costly; they are simply expensive to make.

The three great hunting grounds for these wines are the Rhône, northwest Italy and Australia. By far the easiest to get to grips with is Australia whose rich, full-bodied Cabernets, Grenache and Shiraz wines have a lush sweetness that offsets their intensity. It is sometimes hard to believe that Syrah from the Rhône is the same grape variety. Though full-bodied and spicy, its fruit is much less obvious and the wines often have a slightly gamey quality. Yet its top wines such as Hermitage, Cornas and Côte Rôtie are recognîsed as among the finest in the world.

The great wines of Piedmont in the northwest of Italy, Barolo and Barbaresco, are also quite an acquired taste. Dense, dark and tannic, they can take years to open up. Top Tuscan wines may be less of a challenge, but they are as expensive as top Bordeaux or burgundy.

For everyday drinking, far better value is to be found in the traditional appellations of the Languedoc, such as Corbières, Fitou, Minervois and St-Chinian which blend Syrah with the other classic southern French varieties of Grenache, Mourvèdre and Carignan. Modern Spanish reds such as Jumilla and those from Navarra are also reasonably priced. But for me, the potentially most exciting producer of this style of wine is Portugal, which if it weren't such a slave to old oak casks, could regularly make very fine wines indeed.

Elsewhere in the New World it is Cabernet Sauvignon that provides the most reliable route to this type of drinking, particularly in California where they take it very seriously indeed. Washington State is a newcomer to watch and in the long term Argentina may be able to offer more than Chile. Already its Bonarda, Malbec and Syrah deliver some of the biggest, heftiest wines in the New World.

Finally, there are the bargain basement options: wines that owe little to careful vineyard selection or sophisticated winemaking techniques, but which can provide solid budget drinking. For a barbecue you could do a lot worse than a Rumanian Pinot Noir or a beefy Moroccan red. Not subtle, but they'll probably be appreciated as much by your guests as many a finer, more elegant bottle.

Label clues

A high alcohol content, 13 degrees and over, is obviously the major clue to wines of this style. Wines of 14 degrees will be very big indeed. Look out also for the word "Reserve" on the label, which usually indicates the wine has spent a substantial time in oak and for any mention of old or "bush vines" ("Vieilles Vignes" in French). Also look for unfiltered wines (see pages 26–31).

Above *Châteauneuf-du-Pape is the best-known appellation in the southern Rhône in France, producing potent, spicy, fruity reds.*

Far left *Piedmont in northwest Italy is home to the deeply tannic Nebbiolo grape. Barolo and Barbaresco are the most famous examples of its wines.*

Starting points	
Old World	**New World**
Fitou	Australian Shiraz
Gigondas	Australian and California Cabernet
Châteauneuf-du-Pape	South African Pinotage
Barolo	Zinfandel

BANDOL

Fashionable, small Provençal appellation whose richly flavoured, slightly gamey reds, based on the temperamental Mourvèdre grape, now command hefty prices. The wines, which are aged for at least 18 months in wood should last at least 10 years. ☆☆☆

BARBARESCO

BAROLO's less well-known little sister Barbaresco comes from the same region (Piedmont) and the same grape variety (Nebbiolo) but tends to be lighter and more approachable with less stringent ageing requirements. The region has acquired new prominence as a result of the worldwide fame of its best-known producer Angelo Gaja. ☆☆☆

BAROLO

Despite moves to modernise this famous Italian wine region, this is still one of the most traditionally produced of wines: dark dense and plummy with unfashionably high levels of tannin. Made from the Nebbiolo grape in Piedmont in the northwest of Italy, it often spends three to five years in cask and can take up to 10 years to reach its peak, when it develops a magnificent, deep chocolatey intensity. More expensive wines are labelled with the names of the individual towns or villages they come from: Barolo itself, Castiglione Falletto, La Morra, Monforte and Serralunga. Top wines will also bear the name of an individual vineyard such as La Serra or Cerequio. ☆☆→☆☆☆

BONARDA

Originally a northern Italian grape variety, Bonarda is now achieving some success on its own account in Argentina where it is being used to make big, dense, plummy reds. ☆

BURGUNDY

Although most affordable burgundy is much lighter-bodied than this, the top wines, particularly from the Cote de Nuits, can be intensely rich and concentrated. Among the appellations you will find in this style are **Chassagne-Montrachet, Gevrey-Chambertin** and **Nuits-St-Georges** (though be wary of cheaper versions of both the last two which won't have the same degree of intensity). Premier Cru versions of medium-weight burgundies like **Chambolle-Musigny, Morey-St-Denis, Volnay** and **Vosne-Romanée** are also generally fairly full-bodied. ☆☆☆

CABERNET SAUVIGNON – New World

This grape variety is so widely planted that it is made in a huge variety of styles. The presence of two factors determine whether it is full-bodied or not – a reliably warm or hot climate and the use of oak. Most of the moderately priced and more expensive New World Cabernets from countries such Australia, California and South Africa are full-bodied, as are the top quality Cabernets from Spanish and Italian producers. Only Bordeaux, which is significantly cooler, is consistently made in a drier, smoother style. Full-bodied Cabernets come from:

South Australia Cabernet is grown all over Australia but nowhere does it achieve quite the same concentration and intense, almost jammy sweetness as here. Both the Barossa and McLaren Vale produce some stunning wines, but the top region is Coonawarra whose unique "terra rossa" soil gives its Cabernets a pronounced mint and eucalyptus character resulting in some of the continent's most elegant, long-lived wines. ☆☆→☆☆☆

California Wines made here are more similar to top French Cabernets: partly due to the cooler climate, partly to a conscious decision to ape the winemaking methods of Bordeaux. Nevertheless, there is a an intensity of blackcurrant fruit in the top wines, many of which come from the Napa Valley, that you simply don't find in the Old World. ☆☆→☆☆☆

Washington State A strong pretender to California's throne, this region has already shown the capacity to make some stunningly rich, voluptuous Cabernets (as often as its ferocious winters allow). ☆☆→☆☆☆

Chile While Chile has excelled in producing soft, intensely fruity Cabernets, there is every indication that it will have an equal success in making much more serious wines – but still with that dramatic lush blackcurrant character that distinguishes its cheaper wines. ☆→☆☆

New Zealand The cooler climate here has meant that producers have had difficulty getting Cabernet to ripen, resulting in lean, stalky wines. But improved techniques in the vineyard have resulted in wines with a more typically smooth, blackcurranty character. Even so, New Zealand Cabernet is often blended with Merlot for extra fruitiness. ☆☆→☆☆☆

South Africa Less consistent than some of its fellow New World wine producing countries, but, at the top end of the scale, there are wines of considerable elegance, occasionally with touches of spice and smoke. ☆→☆☆

CAHORS

The reputation of Cahors wines, some of the most full-bodied and tannic in the southwest of France, goes back to the 13th century. Based on the Malbec grape (referred to locally as Auxerrois), they were at one time so dense and dark, they were referred to as "black wine" and were often used to beef up basic Bordeaux. Now blended more extensively with Merlot, many producers are making their wines in a lighter, more supple style. ☆☆

CARIGNAN

A much-despised workhorse of a grape variety planted throughout southern France and the backbone of many of its dark, dense traditional reds, particularly from the LANGUEDOC. However, thanks to the wine retailers' constant search for something new and different to offer the public, it is now undergoing something of a renaissance and is increasingly being bottled as a varietal wine. One of the best versions comes from Sardinia and is called **Carignano del Sulcis**. ☆→☆☆

CHATEAUNEUF-DU-PAPE

The best-known appellation of the southern Rhône, a rich, spicy red based on GRENACHE (though up to 13 different grape varieties

including some whites can be included). Cheaper versions can seem lightweight though deceptively so. The alcohol content is always high.

Better quality wines (which almost invariably come from individual estates and have the papal coat of arms embossed on the bottle) need several years' ageing. Quality is reassuringly consistent. ☆☆→☆☆☆

COLLIOURE

A tiny French appellation, virtually on the Spanish border, producing fine, full, spicy reds based on GRENACHE and Mourvèdre that are among the very best from Roussillon. ☆☆

CORNAS

Small, northern Rhône appellation producing savoury dense long-lived 100 per cent Syrah wines that can compete with HERMITAGE on the opposite bank – and occasionally surpass it for value. ☆☆☆

COTE ROTIE

The most expensive and feted of the Rhône's reds, Côte Rôtie undoubtedly produces some of the most excitingly sensuous wines in the world, combining rich concentration with an extraordinary degree of suppleness. Though predominately made from Syrah, producers may include a small amount of the aromatic white Viognier grape which adds to the wine's heady, seductive bouquet. Scarcity combined with demand has resulted in some frightening prices for these wines. ☆☆☆

Food and occasions

These are obviously not wines that are suited to light, summer drinking, though cheaper bottles can be great with a barbecue. Classic European wines like those from Piedmont and the Rhône go well with substantial French and Italian meat dishes, particularly game or beef. New World Cabernets and Australian Shiraz can handle spicier flavours. All are ideal for warming cold weather food, but are perhaps better saved for fellow red wine enthusiasts than guests whose taste in wine you're unfamiliar with.

DAO

This well-known Portuguese red had a reputation for producing heavily oaked, tannic wines which did little to show off the quality of the indigenous Touriga Nacional grape. But some modernisation is taking place with producers, such as Sogrape, making wines in a much fruitier, more supple style. ☆→☆☆

GRENACHE – old vines

Mature Grenache vines produce wines with an extraordinary degree of concentration, the virtues of which the Australians have belatedly recognised after pulling up some of their oldest vines. Top Californian producer Randall Grahm (of Bonny Doon) is also a fan. ☆☆

HERMITAGE

Arguably the world's most famous full-bodied red and the model for Syrah in both the Old and New World. (Hermitage was the name originally used in Australia for SHIRAZ.) The densest, most concentrated of the northern Rhône appellations, the wines are seldom drinkable under five years and generally better left for 10 or more. ☆☆☆

JUMILLA

A hot, dry area of southern Spain producing rich, dark, high-alcohol reds from the Monastrell (**Mourvèdre**) grape. Traditionally used for blending, more modern winemaking techniques have resulted in some attractively lush, fruity wines. ☆→☆☆

LANGUEDOC – traditional

Though they are made over a wide geographical area, there is a strong family resemblance between the reds of the Languedoc, with differences frequently being more marked between one producer and another than between appellations. The most robust wines are from poorer schistous soils and producers who use a higher proportion of CARIGNAN: primarily the **Fitou** and **St-Chinian** areas. Other producers who use a higher proportion of GRENACHE, Syrah and Mourvèdre such as those in the **Faugères** and **Minervois**, generally make lighter, more elegant wines. **Corbières**, the biggest region, produces a wide range of styles but many producers still age their wines for some considerable time in oak which makes them among the more full-bodied choices.

Things change fast in the Languedoc, though, due to the combination of lack of regulation and the large number of foreign winemakers working in the region. Many of the more ambitious and dynamic producers are now electing to produce their wines as **Coteaux du Languedoc** rather than one of the more traditional appellations. Up-and-coming areas to look out for are **Montpeyroux**, **La Clape** and **Pic St-Loup**. ☆→☆☆

MADIRAN

A traditionally full-bodied wine based on the tannic Tannat grape produced to the south of Armagnac, not far from the Spanish border. In recent years the proportion of Tannat has been reduced and that of CABERNET SAUVIGNON and Cabernet Franc increased, creating more elegant and approachable wines. ☆☆

MOROCCO

Vine growing was part of the French legacy to Morocco, but the industry has never really developed. It is, however, a source of some good, gutsy, inexpensive reds, particularly those made from the Syrah grape. ☆

NAVARRA

One of the fastest developing of Spain's wine growing regions, Navarra's reds, many of which contain CABERNET SAUVIGNON, are made in a much more modern, international style than is typical for the country. ☆☆

PERIQUITA – and other Portuguese reds

Portugal has huge potential as a red wine producing country, not least because its wines are so individual. Quantum leaps in winemaking techniques are already resulting in the production of some fine, characterful, full-bodied reds from local grape varieties such as Periquita, Touriga Nacional, Touriga Francesca and Tinta Roriz (Spain's Tempranillo). Progress has been most marked in the **Alentejo** and **Douro** regions though even more traditional regions like **Bairrada** and DAO are making more accessible wines. ☆→☆☆

PINOTAGE

This indigenous South African grape, a blend of PINOT NOIR and Cinsault, is capable of making magnificently dense, plummy wines when made from low-yielding old vines. Best examples represent tremendous value. ☆☆

PINOT NOIR – Romanian

Although Pinot Noir would not generally be thought of as a full-bodied wine, the variety planted in Romania, the Burgund Mare, makes hefty, brambly reds of no great subtlety or distinction, but at an exceptionally modest price. ☆

ST-JOSEPH

One of the more affordable, approachable (and variable) of the northern Rhône Syrahs, lacking the density and concentration of its weightier neighbours, but, in the hands of top producers, still a full-bodied wine by any standards. ☆☆☆

SHIRAZ

Although light, fruity versions of Shiraz exist, Australian Shiraz has made its reputation as a powerhouse grape. It is capable of producing fabulously concentrated wines that at their best rival the Syrah produced in the Rhône. The most intense character, with its distinctive black pepper spice, is realised in the hot, arid vineyards of South Australia, particularly the Barossa Valley, where old vines and low yields combine to produce wines of intense character and concentration (though Australia's best known Shiraz, **Grange**, has more in common with Bordeaux, particularly when aged).

Hunter Valley Shiraz has a different character, developing more animal, gamey notes, sometimes described as "sweaty saddle", while Shiraz from cooler Western Australia is a much tamer creature altogether, with smooth red berry fruit, not unlike a CABERNET. An increasing amount of Shiraz is also being produced in South Africa. ☆☆→☆☆☆

VINO NOBILE DE MONTEPULCIANO

A smooth, sophisticated Tuscan wine made primarily from the Sangiovese grape. A cheaper alternative to **Brunello di Montalcino**. ☆☆

ZINFANDEL

Like SHIRAZ, Zinfandel can be light and jammy, but in the hands of small artisanal winemakers produces wines of great power and personality which have attracted something of a cult following. Established in California during the last century, it is believed to be related to the Italian grape Primitivo, and shares its exuberant brambly fruit. The best growing areas are in Northern California in the Dry Creek and Alexander Valleys, the Sierra Foothills and Paso Robles to the south of San Francisco which still retain many old vines. A small amount is also grown in South Africa and Western Australia. ☆☆→☆☆☆

Storing and serving

Most full-bodied wines will survive for at least a couple of years in average domestic conditions and in the case of more expensive wines, a good five to eight years. Some like the top Rhône and Italian wines need that amount of time before they even start to be drinkable. Open them at least an hour, preferably two before serving them, or even decant them beforehand.

AGED RED WINES AND RARITIES

One of the biggest changes in the wine world is how soon we now drink a bottle of red wine after we've bought it. Traditionally, any remotely serious red wine was always "laid down" and no-one would have dreamt of drinking it young. Nowadays, even expensive wines are designed to be drunk straight off the shelf with the result that the taste of mature wine is quite unfamiliar, not to say unappealing, to many wine drinkers.

The taste is indeed very different. Instead of the vivid fruit and robust tannins of a young wine, the texture and flavour become softer and less assertive. Simple blackcurrant or raspberry fruit gives way to the more autumnal flavours of prunes and plums, and even all kinds of unlikely aromas and flavours. A mature burgundy, for example, can have distinctly "farmyardy" aromas, a smell of wet undergrowth, or frequently of truffles or mushrooms, a quality much prized by burgundy aficionados, but one that can come as quite a shock first time around.

Wine lives and breathes

Why this change occurs is that unlike other packaged food and drink products wine continues evolving in the bottle. After bottling there is always a small amount of oxygen left which reacts with the phenols in the wine (the compounds in the stems, skins and pips and pulp of grapes which give wine colour and structure) which eventually cluster together to form a sediment which drops to the bottom of the bottle. (This is why older red wines fade in colour and become less tannic.)

Of course this doesn't happen to all wines – or all wines at the same rate. Fruity, unoaked reds that are designed to be drunk young, simply become dull and flat tasting. There's no point in keeping a Beaujolais Nouveau. Some grapes age better than others: Syrah and Shiraz, for example, will generally outlive Pinot Noir. Cabernet Sauvignon has more staying power than Merlot. But even Cabernet varies in its capacity to age depending on where and how it is made (see listing).

In cooler regions, such as Bordeaux and Burgundy, the longevity of a wine also relates to the quality of the vintage. In a good year like 1995, the grapes ripen fully and the resulting wines are more concentrated and age better than thinner wines of a poor year like 1991 or 1992.

But the most significant factor is how concentrated a wine is in the first place – and that is almost always reflected in its price. As a general rule, cheaper wines age more quickly than expensive ones, as do wines produced by more traditional wine areas like Bulgaria, Spain and Portugal, which age more quickly than similar New World wines. Partly this reflects the type of oak that is used. Wine aged in old oak casks will taste more obviously woody than wine that is aged in new oak barrels which impart a lusher texture and a more lively vanilla flavour.

In fact, people are more likely to come to grief from letting wines age for too long than by drinking them too quickly. In centrally heated flats and houses, wines rarely benefit from being kept for more than two or three years. It is only so-called "fine wines" that are worth keeping for any longer than that – and that assumes ideal storage conditions (*see* pages 110–113). Among them would be included wines from Bordeaux, Burgundy and the Rhône, more expensive Italian reds from Tuscany and Piedmont and top wines from California and Australia. Many won't even begin to show at their best for five years or more.

That doesn't mean if you have a taste for mature wine but are without a pocket to match that you can't indulge yourself. Spain, in particular, is a good hunting ground for reasonably priced oak-aged reds, most notably Rioja, but inexpensive examples also come from Conca de Barbera, La Mancha, Penedès and Valdepeñas. The same is true of wines like Copertino and Salice Salentino from southern Italy. But buy them straight off the shelf, don't store them for years yourself.

Also included here are some of the wine world's most quirky and individual reds – wines like Aglianico del Vulture and the great Lebanese wine Château Musar. Given their rarity, they are very reasonable, but not to everyone's taste. Save them for fellow enthusiasts.

Label clues

The most obvious indication that a wine is mature is that it comes from an older vintage, but unless you are confident of your source be wary of buying any inexpensive or moderately priced wine over five years old. Look out for the words "Reserve", "Riserva" or "Reserva" which indicate an oak-aged wine intended to be matured.

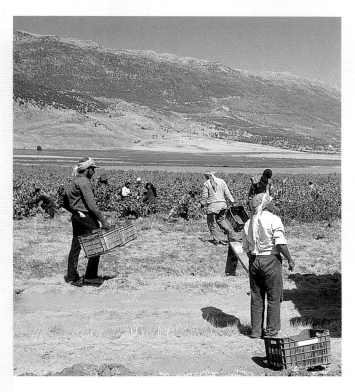

Above *Harvesting at Château Musar – the finest Lebanese wine – a rich, full-bodied blend of Cabernet Sauvignon, Cinsaut and Syrah.*

Far left *A classic image to make any wine lover start to salivate and think recklessly about their bank balance.*

Starting points	
Aged wines	**Rarities**
Bulgarian Cabernet Sauvignon	Amarone
Valdepeñas	Aglianico del Vulture
Copertino	Château Musar
Rioja Reserva or Gran Reserva	

AGLIANICO DEL VULTURE

One of the lesser-known but great full-bodied Italian reds made down in the very south of Italy from the late-ripening Aglianico grape. ☆☆ → ☆☆☆

AMARONE

A unique off-dry, almost port-like red of great richness and concentration made in the Valpolicella region in northeastern Italy from the local Corvina, Rondinella and Molinara grape varieties. It can be drunk with rich meat and game dishes but with at least 14 degrees of alcohol is probably more suitable as an accompaniment for cheese. ☆☆ → ☆☆☆

BARCA VELHA

Cult Portuguese red from the Douro region, made from the same grape varieties as port (from the same region). It is released only in an exceptional year. ☆☆☆

BORDEAUX – Crus Classés

Not all of the 61 wines of the officially recognised top growths of the Médoc qualify for this section on grounds of rarity, but the fact is that most of us will get to drink a wine like Château Latour or Mouton Rothschild once in a lifetime – if that. Certainly it's worth being able to recognise the names of the five first growths – **Haut-Brion**, **Lafite-Rothschild**, **Latour**, **Margaux**, and **Mouton-Rothschild** – together with the two Pomerol superstars, **Chateaux Pétrus** and

Le Pin – so you can appreciate just what you're being offered if anyone opens one up for you. But the lesser growths – indicated by the words, "Deuxième", "Troisième", "Quatrième" or "Cinquième Cru" – offer better value. ☆☆☆

BRUNELLO DI MONTALCINO

An elegant and expensive Tuscan wine, Italy's equivalent to the top Bordeaux growths is made from Brunello, a variant of the Sangiovese grape. Like other top Italian reds, it spends a substantial time in oak and isn't released until it is at least four years old. Good vintages will last for decades. ☆☆☆

CABERNET SAUVIGNON – mature

Because of its basically tough, tannic character Cabernet Sauvignon is one of the grape varieties best suited to ageing, as top winemakers have amply demonstrated in both the Old and the New World. The rate at which this happens, however, differs quite markedly. Wines that age quickly include those from Bulgaria and Spain which will develop the typically soft, pruney flavour of mature Cabernet within three to four years of bottling. But more expensive Australian and Californian Cabernets which have an intense concentration of fruit, may not develop that kind of character for eight to 10 years. ☆☆ → ☆☆☆

CHATEAU MUSAR

The most distinguished red wine of the Lebanon which continued to be produced throughout the civil war. This is a long lived,

powerful, yet elegant blend of Cabernet Sauvignon, Cinsault and Syrah, which bears comparison with many far more expensive BORDEAUX wines. ☆☆

CHIANTI CLASSICO RISERVA

The ageing requirements for Chianti Classico and other Riserva Chiantis have now been reduced from three to two years, but Riservas should still be significantly longer-living than basic Chianti. The top wines from such producers as Antinori and Isole e Olena can age for up to 30 years. ☆☆ → ☆☆☆

GARRAFEIRA – Portugal

An indication of quality in Portuguese wines denoting that the wine is from an exceptional vintage, has been aged for two years in oak and for a further year in the bottle. ☆☆

GRANGE

Australia's most sought after Shiraz, a wine first produced in the 1950s (as Grange Hermitage) in an attempt to emulate BORDEAUX's first growths. It does, in fact, taste more like a mature CABERNET SAUVIGNON. ☆☆☆

NEGROAMARO

Southern Italian reds have a particularly distinctive flavour that means that even when they're young they taste like a well-matured wine. You can almost taste the hot sun in the wines: there's a kind of baked, caramelised

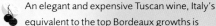

flavour to them saved from being bitter by a delicious brown sugar fudginess. Most are based on the Negroamaro (literally "black and bitter") grape combined with Malvasia Nera. Names to look out for include **Copertino**, **Salice Salentino** and **Squinzano**. ☆→☆☆

PRIORATO

A small denomination in the Spanish province of Catalonia producing intensely concentrated, alcoholic wines (the minimum alcohol content is 13.75) from low-yielding Garnacha (Grenache) and Cariñena (Carignan) vines. ☆☆☆

RIBERA DEL DUERO

Ribera del Duero has taken over from Rioja as Spain's most prestigious red wine producing region, with two of its wines **Vega Sicilia** and **Pesquera** achieving cult status. Based on a blend of Tempranillo (called Tinto Fino in Ribera), CABERNET SAUVIGNON and Merlot and aged for at least three (and more commonly five or six years in oak). The top wines are intensely rich and concentrated and drink well for 20 years or more. ☆☆→☆☆☆

RIOJA RESERVA/GRAN RESERVA

Prolonged ageing in oak makes mature Reserva and Gran Reserva Rioja some of the most obviously oaky wines available, their typical soft strawberry jam fruit giving way over time to more complex gamey flavours.

Reserva indicates that the wine will have been aged for three years before release, at least one of which will have been spent in oak; Gran Reserva is only released after five years, two of them in oak. This classification system is also used for other Spanish reds such as those from Navarra. ☆☆→☆☆☆

LA ROMANEE-CONTI

The production of Burgundy's most celebrated wines like La Romanée-Conti, **Richebourg** and **La Tâche** is so minute that almost every bottle is spoken for before the grapes are harvested (La Romanée-Conti is a single vineyard less than two hectares in size). There are other Grands Crus such as **Bonnes Mares**, **Corton** and **Echézeaux** which are easier to get hold of – if you can afford them. ☆☆☆

SASSICAIA – and other Super Tuscans

A group of top Tuscan wines of great depth and extraction, made from non-traditional grape varieties such as CABERNET SAUVIGNON and ostentatiously labelled "Vino da Tavola" to demonstrate disregard for the constraints of the DOC system. The best-known are Sassicaia, **Ornellaia** and **Tignanello**. (Sassicaia now has its own denomination Sassicaia Bolgheri while the others may be reclassified under the new denomination of Toscana.) ☆☆☆

VALDEPENAS

A reasonably priced source of typically Spanish style oak-aged reds, made primarily from Tempranillo (called Cencibel in this region). Drink at three to four years old. ☆→☆☆

Food and occasions

It is unwise (as well as a waste) to serve up a very old or unusual wine unless you know your guests will enjoy it. You also need to be careful about the kind of food you serve. The delicate flavours of mature wines need complementary rather than competing flavours which are more likely to be found in plainly cooked, classic dishes.

Storing and serving

The older a wine gets, the more carefully you should treat it. Older bottles may throw a sediment. Leave them upright 24 hours before serving and don't open them too far in advance. Wines that are full-bodied and still likely to be tannic can benefit from decanting.

ROSE WINES

Rosé suffers from its frothy, frivolous image. It is seen as the kind of wine that no self-respecting wine drinker, particularly male, would be seen dead with. But in many parts of Europe it is a way of life. Far more rosé is drunk than white and there's nothing unmanly or wimpish about it.

The colour of rosé of course comes from red grapes, so it is a logical by-product of areas like Bordeaux or the Languedoc which mainly produce red wine. There are a number of different ways of making it, although it is not a question of mixing white and red wine.

One method is simply to press the grapes and immediately run off the juice which is barely coloured by its contact with the grape skins. Another, the "saignée" method, is to leave just-crushed grapes to macerate together for 24 to 48 hours and then run off the juice ("saignée" means bleed) which by now will have picked up quite a deep colour.

The important thing, both for colour and flavour, is how long the juice remains in contact with the skins. If it is only brief you will get a pale pink colour and a delicate fruit flavour. When extended, the result is darker and gutsier. But part of the charm of rosés is this variation in colour from the delicate onion-skin, pinky beige colour, through candyfloss pink, to rich, golden salmon and almost reddish magenta.

Versatile summer drinking

Almost all parts of southern Europe produce a simple rosé for everyday drinking. Light, low in alcohol, it is perfect for warm weather. But there are more serious rosés, notably from Provence, the southern Rhône and Bordeaux. In Provence, rosé has become positively fashionable; wines from appellations like Bandol and Bellet command prices as high as their red and white counterparts. Tavel, in the southern Rhône produces a full-bodied, alcoholic rosé which stands up to the same robust foods as a red.

More widely available are Bordeaux rosés (often called "clairet") which provide particularly elegant drinking. And there is more to offer from the Loire than the rather dull sweetish rosés like Rosé d'Anjou. Try Rosé de Loire and Cabernet d'Anjou which are made in a drier, crisper style or the rosés from red wine areas such as Chinon and Bourgueil.

If you prefer a more robust, rustic style of rosé the best hunting grounds are Spain's *rosados* and the traditional wines of the Languedoc – certainly the wines to drink if you visit the region. Taste them with your eyes closed and you could almost be drinking a light red.

Rosés don't feature as strongly in the New World, but the few wines that are produced are made from a single grape variety, the most favoured being Grenache, Shiraz and Cabernet Sauvignon. Like New World reds, they tend to be much richer, sweeter and fruitier than their European counterparts, much higher in alcohol and lower in acidity.

This New World approach has reached the more dynamic, forward-looking areas of Europe. You find good crisp dry Cabernet rosés, for example, from Hungary and gutsy Syrah rosés from the Languedoc.

The exception to general New World rule is California which pioneered and has had great success with "blush" wines: light coloured, medium-sweet rosés that have provided an easy starting point for many new wine drinkers. Rather than being described as rosé, they are marketed as "White", the most popular of which being White Zinfandel. On the whole, though, the slightly sweeter style of rosé popularised by Mateus Rosé and Rosé d'Anjou is in decline among wine drinkers who have moved on to the more robustly fruity wines of the New World.

In the end though, drinking rosé is a question of having the confidence not to be put off by what other people might think and to simply enjoy drinking a uniquely refreshing style of wine. Ironically the style of rosé that is taken most seriously in the wine world is rosé with bubbles, i.e. pink champagne, and there's nothing frothier than that.

Label clues

As with other still wines, one of the best clues to the style of a rosé is alcohol content. Lighter rosés will tend to be 11–11.5 degrees, more robust ones up to 13. The colour is also a giveaway. The darker the wine the more full-bodied and fruity it is likely to be. As rosé should be drunk as fresh as possible, make sure it comes from the most recent vintage.

Above *California is one of the largest producers of rosé ("blush") wines. In this vineyard, the frames help to train the vines in a way that gives the grapes maximum exposure to the sun.*

Far left *Rosé drinking is an integral part of the French way of life in Provence and other parts of southern France, where it is more popular than white wine.*

Starting points	
Dry, crisp and elegant	**Full-bodied/rustic**
Bordeaux	Spanish Rosado
Bandol	Languedoc Rosé
Marsannay	Tavel
New World flavours	**Light/Medium dry**
Cabernet Sauvignon Rosé	Rosé d'Anjou
Grenache Rosé	Mateus Rosé
Syrah/Shiraz Rosé	Lambrusco Rosé

BARDOLINO CHIARETTO

 An attractive light, cherry flavoured rosé from the northern Italian region of Bardolino, near Lake Garda. ✩✩

BERGERAC ROSE

 A pretty strawberry flavoured rosé from the Dordogne region in southwest France, less high profile but produced in a very similar style to BORDEAUX. Worth looking out for. ✩✩

"BLUSH"

 A term originated in the late 1980s in California as a brilliant marketing device to resuscitate declining sales of rosé. It is now widely used elsewhere in the world to indicate a light, usually slightly sweetish style of rosé. ✩

BORDEAUX

 Rosé production is on the increase in Bordeaux. In fact producers such as Château de Sours and Château Méaume make some of the most elegant rosés on the market, predominantly from MERLOT, rather than the more traditional CABERNET SAUVIGNON. They are bone dry, but full-flavoured with lovely light soft raspberry fruit. ✩✩

CABERNET SAUVIGNON

 As you might expect, Cabernet Sauvignon makes a dry, crisp, full-bodied style of rosé with a characteristic blackcurrant note to the

fruit. It's been a popular choice among flying winemakers working in Hungary and is proving increasingly popular in Chile. ✩→✩✩

CINSAULT

 Cinsault is widely used throughout the LANGUEDOC and PROVENCE for rosé. It is often blended with GRENACHE to make a particularly robust full-bodied style of wine. ✩→✩✩

CLAIRET

 Nearer to a light red than a rosé, Clairet, which was the origin of the word claret, has been produced in BORDEAUX for years and actually has its own appellation. It is not generally as distinguished as Bordeaux rosé. ✩✩

GRENACHE

 A popular grape variety among winemakers in both the Old and New World for producing full-bodied, intense, often dark coloured rosés. It is the basis for PROVENCE's best-known rosé **Tavel** and for Australian producer Geoff Merrill's particularly robust style of rosé under the Mount Hurtle label. In California it is made in a sweeter style and bottled as **White Grenache**. ✩→✩✩

LAMBRUSCO

 A very light, bland, sweetish rosé, mainly produced for export markets. Low alcohol versions are made too, though these are generally poor. ✩

LANGUEDOC ROSE

 Like the other still wines of the Languedoc, its rosé is made in two styles. There are the brightly fruity, New World style rosés made from single grape varieties like CABERNET and SYRAH and the more traditional, drier, crisper wines made by small producers from local grapes such as GRENACHE, CINSAUT and Carignan. ✩→✩✩

LOIRE ROSE

 Bland and almost invariably oversweetened, **Rosé d'Anjou**, made from the undistinguished Grolleau grape, is usually one of the least exciting rosés. Considerably better are the drier, more elegant **Rosé de Loire** and **Cabernet d'Anjou** which are generally made from Cabernet Franc. **Bourgueil** and **Chinon** also make very good rosé, though it is by no means cheap. ✩✩→✩✩✩

MATEUS ROSE

 This famous sweetish slightly fizzy rosé, in its distinctive round bottle, was a common starting point for many wine drinkers in the 1960s and 1970s. Since then its popularity has declined, but, it's a rather better drink than other popular off-dry rosés like WHITE ZIN. ✩✩

MERLOT

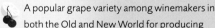 Not a traditional grape variety for rosé, but increasingly popular because of its particularly attractive ripe red berry fruit. It is used in the United States to make **White Merlot**. ✩→✩✩

MOURVEDRE

 The vogue for Mourvèdre has rubbed off on the elegant stylish rosés that are made from this grape variety, particularly in PROVENCE. ☆☆→☆☆☆

PINOT NOIR

 One of the most successful varieties for rosé making some of the prettiest, most delicately fruity rosés around. The best examples are **Marsannay** from Burgundy and **Sancerre Rosé** which has a distinctive pale strawberry red colour, but good rosés are also produced in lesser-known **St-Pourcain**. ☆→☆☆☆

PROVENCE ROSE

 Provence is the region most associated with rosé drinking, though its fashionability often means the quality of the wines doesn't quite live up to their price. Most are made from a blend of GRENACHE and CINSAULT, labelled as **Côtes de Provence**, and are rarely more than refreshing light, quaffing wines. More ambitious, stylish wines from small appellations such as **Bandol**, **Cassis** and **Palette** tend also to include MOURVEDRE. ☆☆→☆☆☆

ROSADO – Spain

 Rosé drinking is a way of life for large parts of Spain, particularly in Navarra and Rioja. Most are based on GRENACHE (Garnarcha) and have an endearingly robust, rustic quality, but there are individual producers such as Chivite who produce wines of real elegance. ☆→☆☆

SYRAH

 A grape variety increasingly favoured (especially among the the new generation of winemakers in the LANGUEDOC) for producing full flavoured, fruity rosés with a characteristic Syrah spiciness. A particularly exuberant version is produced by Balbi in Argentina. ☆→☆☆

TAVEL

 This most famous of French rosés (the appellation makes nothing else) comes from the southern Rhône. Predominantly made from GRENACHE it has always been quite heavy and alcoholic and rarely benefits from being kept as long as some of the winemakers recommend. Some producers are now moving to a lighter style more similar to that of neighbouring **Lirac**. ☆☆→☆☆☆

VIN GRIS

 A pale type of rosé made by leaving the juice in minimum contact with the skins. The best known example is **Listel Gris de Gris**, made down on the Mediterranean coast. ☆→☆☆

WHITE ZINFANDEL

 Although it is called white, White Zin, as it is affectionately known is in fact a rosé made from the Zinfandel grape. Light, sweet and slightly fizzy, it has proved hugely popular with the wine drinking public since it was first launched in California in the late 1980s. ☆→☆☆

Food and occasions

Rosé is the ultimate seasonal wine, tailor-made for summer and particularly outdoor eating. It is the perfect wine to take on a picnic or for an al fresco supper in the garden. It is also very flexible with food. Its naturally high acidity makes it an ideal partner for sharply dressed salads, particularly those made with tomato.

Storing and serving

Don't even think about laying rosé down. You should drink it as soon as possible after you've bought it. Treat it like a dry white wine and serve it well chilled.

CHAMPAGNE AND SPARKLING WINE

Most people are not aware of the differences in style among sparkling wines. It's more a question of image. If it's an occasion where we want to make an impression we go for champagne. If it's less important we are prepared to consider a sparkler. What is uppermost in most people's minds is not what the wine actually tastes like, but whether it has a label that other people will recognise.

Such an approach fails to recognise what has been going on over the last few years. A decade ago the champagne producers had the quality sparkling wine market to themselves. Now places like California and New Zealand rival them for quality, often, ironically, with the help of those self same champagne producers who have seen the opportunity to make fine wines in the New World and set up their own base there.

The New World has also shown a growing self-confidence about making wines that are not in the style of champagne, wines that are less elegant certainly, but much smoother, fruitier and easier to drink. All this innovation has had a knock-on effect on the quality of champagne itself. These days you see far fewer thin, sharp, acidic champagnes and far more with a smoother, fuller flavour.

Sparkling wine production is best suited to the cooler wine regions of the world, though few are as cool as champagne itself. Whereas most winemakers' primary concern is how ripe they can get their grapes, a champagne or sparkling wine producer is actually looking for a high level of acidity, though in a poor year there is the option of blending in a richer-flavoured wine from previous vintages.

Dark skinned grape varieties

It may come as a surprise, given that champagne is a white wine, that two of the grape varieties regularly used in its production are the dark skinned Pinot Noir and Pinot Meunier. The third is Chardonnay which can also be used on its own (this is called a Blanc de Blancs). The variations in style between one champagne and another often reflect the proportions of these grapes the producer uses. More Chardonnay and you get a lighter, more elegant style. More Pinot Noir and you have a champagne that will be richer and more full-bodied.

This lengthy, labour-intensive process helps to explain why champagne and wines and similar methods (notably "méthode traditionelle") are so expensive. Significantly cheaper sparkling wines are generally made in a huge tank and then bottled under pressure.

They lack the complexity of champagne but the method is perfectly suited to grape varieties like Moscato (Muscat) where a simple fragrance and flavour is what is wanted.

Undoubtedly you pay a premium for the champagne name, so if you enjoy drinking sparkling wine for its own sake rather than just for a celebration, it's worth exploring outside the region for a style that appeals. In France the main area of sparkling wine production is the Loire though there is also some produced in Alsace, Burgundy and a small pocket around Limoux in the south of France. The Spanish have their crisp, dry Cava, while the Italians have a strong tradition of producing semi-sweet *spumante* wines from the Muscat grape.

But it has been in the New World that the biggest challenge to champagne has come, particularly where the champenois themselves have set up shop. The highest quality is to be found in California and New Zealand, though it is Australia – never afraid to break with convention and do its own thing – that offers the widest choice of prices and styles, including a spectacularly fruity style of red sparkling wine. South Africa, though it doesn't always deliver on quality, can also provide very good full-bodied, rich tasting wines.

Label clues

It is simple to tell whether a champagne is non-vintage or vintage. Only vintage champagne actually gives the year on the label. The other clue to style is the word "Brut" which indicates that it is made in a dry style. The terms "Sec" or "Demi-Sec" mean off-dry or medium-sweet.

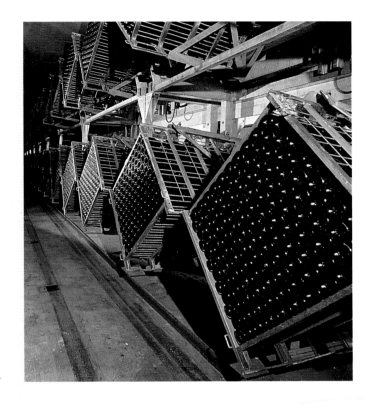

Above *Gyropalattes are a mechanical method of performing the traditional task of riddling – turning the bottles of sparkling wine so that the lees (yeast deposits) end up in the neck of the bottle and can be disposed of.*

Far left *The pastoral countryside of the Champagne region in northeast France – an area whose still wines were generally so harsh that an ingenious method was devised to make them more enjoyable. This is now referred to as the "méthode traditionelle".*

Starting points	
Light and creamy	**Rich and toasty**
Sparkling Chardonnay	Top New Zealand sparkling wine
Crémant de Bourgogne	Top Californian sparkling wine
Blanc de Blancs champagne	Grand Marque NV champagne
	Vintage champagne
Dry, crisp and yeasty	**Medium-dry**
Cava	Moscato d'Asti
Saumur Brut	Asti Spumante
Inexpensive NV champagne	Demi-Sec champagne

BLANC DE BLANCS

 Literally a white wine made from white grapes, this description indicates that the champagne has been made from Chardonnay alone. As a result it is likely to be lighter, creamier and less toasty than one made from a high proportion of Pinot Noir and Pinot Meunier. ☆☆→☆☆☆

BLANC DE NOIRS

 Far less common than BLANC DE BLANCS this means a champagne made only from dark skinned grapes (Pinot Noir and Pinot Meunier) and which is consequently likely to be more full-bodied. ☆☆→☆☆☆

BRUT

 The term used to indicate that a champagne is dry. A few very dry champagnes are labelled "**ultra brut**", though strangely, "**extra brut**" is not as dry as brut. ☆→☆☆

DEMI-SEC

 Confusingly the term used to describe a sweet champagne is demi-sec (literally half-dry), though in most cases the wine will be sweet enough to drink with a dessert. More recently some producers (including Veuve Clicquot and Roederer) have introduced a category called "**rich**" – which is exactly that: sweeter than normal but luscious and full-bodied too. It can be drunk with equally rich savoury dishes like *foie gras*. ☆☆→☆☆☆

DOUX

 The term for a sweet style of champagne intended for drinking with desserts. Currently not as fashionable as the newly launched "**rich**" styles (*see* DEMI-SEC). ☆☆→☆☆☆

GRAND CRU

 In Champagne this means that the grapes have come from a vineyard officially designated Grand Cru. But, in fact, the wine may not necessarily be of such high quality as a PRESTIGE CUVEE. ☆☆☆

MAGNUM

Champagne that is bottled in a magnum (1.5 litres) generally ages better than a standard sized bottle resulting in a richer, fuller-tasting fizz. There is also the element of show. It always seems much more impressive to serve up one large bottle than two small ones – and it generally costs little more. ☆☆→☆☆☆

METHODE TRADITIONELLE

The way champagne is produced (called the *méthode champenoise* within the Champagne region, Méthode Traditionelle outside it) also gives the wine its distinctive flavour. Once the winemaker has blended the different individual components of his wine (which are drawn from different vineyards and different years) sugar and yeast are added and the resulting wine is actually fermented in the bottle, creating the carbon dioxide that is finally released as bubbles when the cork pops. This fermentation process creates a residue, the lees, which enriches the flavour of the champagne as it lies in the bottle. The longer the champagne stays in contact with its lees the better. Less than 18 months and it won't develop that typical yeasty, biscuity character that makes champagne so distinctive.

The final step is that the bottle is gradually up-ended (traditionally by hand, increasingly by machine) so that the yeast residues are deposited in the neck of the bottle. Then the neck of the bottle is quickly frozen, the residue discarded and the bottle topped up with a sweetened wine (called the *dosage*) which is adjusted depending on how sweet the winemaker wants the final wine to be.

NON-VINTAGE

 The term non-vintage has negative connotations, implying that it's second best to VINTAGE champagne. But, in fact, it refers more to the way the champagne is made, blending wine from different vintages in order to achieve a consistent style. Nevertheless, a non-vintage champagne is likely to contain a higher proportion of young wine and so the style is likely to be dry, fresh and crisp, with a more or less yeasty, toasty or honeyed character depending on how long it has been left on its lees (*see* above).

Most of the well-known brands, or **Grandes Marques** as they are known in Champagne, will have been aged for two to three years, though the minimum requirement is only 12 months. So there is a world of difference in style between a cut-price champagne which may taste quite thin and acidic and the non-vintage champagne of a Grande Marque like Bollinger or a highly regarded independent producer such as Billecart-Salmon. There are also champagne producers who cultivate a distinctive house style. Taittinger, for example, uses a high proportion of Chardonnay to produce a particularly light, elegant style of champagne. Veuve Clicquot is rich and full-bodied. ☆→☆☆

RECEMMENT DEGORGE

 This term means a mature wine that has been recently bottled giving it a particularly fresh, elegant flavour. Only the house of Bollinger has the right to use the initials RD as an abbreviation (the house has registered "RD" as a trademark). ☆☆☆

RECOLTANT-MANIPULANT

You can tell if a wine is a grower's champagne by the initials RM (recoltant-manipulant) on the label. Although the French like to buy their champagne direct from their favourite grower, it's a rather more hazardous enterprise if you live outside the country. As a small grower hasn't got the same range of grapes or reserves of old wine to call on as the big champagne houses, quality can fluctuate from one year to another, so it's better to go through a specialist wine merchant who knows his suppliers. ☆→☆☆

ROSE

 Rosé champagne is taken far more seriously than still rosé wines, with several houses actually producing vintage versions. Some are produced like other rosés by leaving the juice in contact with dark coloured grape skins, others by adding a little red wine to the blend before the second fermentation takes place. ☆→☆☆☆

PRESTIGE CUVEE

 A term used by champagne producers to describe their best VINTAGE champagnes. Well known examples are Dom Pérignon, Roederer Cristal, Veuve Cliquot La Grande Dame and Bollinger RD. Many houses are also releasing special Millennium cuvées. ☆☆☆

VINTAGE

 Vintage champagne comes from a single, exceptional year so it should in theory be richer, toastier, and generally fuller flavoured than a NON-VINTAGE champagne. But that isn't a taste that necessarily appeals to all wine drinkers, some of whom may actually prefer a lighter style. Over time (and it will last for several years) it can acquire quite a mature "cellary" kind of character particularly if, like Krug, it is aged in oak. ☆☆→☆☆☆

Food and occasions

Although you may still feel that you should serve champagne for a celebration these days you don't have to. What's more important is to tailor the style of wine to the occasion. If it's a stand-up party or reception with canapés or finger food, go for a lighter wine. If it's a special dinner where you will be drinking sparkling wine throughout the meal go for a richer, fuller-flavoured style. In fact, champagne and other sparkling wines are surprisingly flexible with food. The only combinations that can be tricky are dry champagne with a rich dessert that emphasises its acidity and hot spicy dishes (though both Chinese and Japanese food can work well). Sweeter sparklers like Doux and Demi-Sec champagne and Asti can be delicious with fruit-based desserts and cakes, while red sparklers are an adventurous choice for a barbecue.

ASTI

In spite of the fact that it has been renamed Asti, Asti Spumante is still the name by which most people know this best selling medium-dry wine. On these grounds alone it tends to be looked down on, although drunk in the right context (on a warm summer's day), the refreshingly grapey end result can be far more enjoyable than wine snobs admit. ☆

AUSTRALIAN

Given its warmer than average climate, it is not surprising that many Australian sparkling wines are more obviously fruity and less acidic than their European counterparts. Most provide uncomplicated, good value drinking. But there are a handful of producers, such as Domaine Chandon who are producing more ambitiously elegant wines. ☆→☆☆

BLANQUETTE DE LIMOUX

This soft, creamy, slightly appley sparkler from the Languedoc reputedly pre-dates champagne. It is made primarily from the local Mauzac grape together with some Chenin Blanc and CHARDONNAY. ☆→☆☆

CAP CLASSIQUE

This is the term used in South Africa to describe sparkling wines made by the traditional champagne method. The country shows considerable promise as a sparkling wine producer, frequently releasing more complex rich, toasty wines than Australia, though not generally of the same consistently high standard as California or New Zealand. ☆☆

CAVA

Cava, which comes from Spain, is the great sparkling wine success story of recent years producing consistently good, straightforward, dry, yeasty sparkling wine at an exceptionally reasonable price. Vintage Cava isn't always such good value.☆→☆☆

CHARDONNAY

An increasingly popular grape for New World sparkling wines, though with more of a creamy vanilla soda flavour than the tropical fruit character associated with this grape. ☆→☆☆

CLAIRETTE DE DIE

A little-known delicately sweet French sparkling wine from the Rhône Valley. There is also a **Crémant de Die** which is similar in style. ☆

CREMANT DE BOURGOGNE

With the same grapes as champagne (CHARDONNAY and Pinot Noir) and only a slightly warmer climate, Burgundy seems a natural area to make *crémant* – the word the French use outside Champagne for sparkling wine. And although not as fine or as complex, it can be very good. Other *crémants* to look for include **Crémant d'Alsace** and **Crémant de Loire**, which, because they don't carry the champagne name, can be excellent value. ☆☆

MOSCATO D'ASTI

This softly sparkling off-dry wine is similar in style and produced in the same region (the northwest of Italy) as ASTI but tends to be of better quality. It is also marvellously low in alcohol (5.5 degrees). ☆

MUMM CUVEE NAPA

The best-known of the increasing number of quality California sparklers made with technical input and financial investment from champagne houses. Indeed many of the top cuvées like Roederer's Quartet and Jordan's "J" exceed a lot of basic champagne in quality. ☆☆→☆☆☆

NEW ZEALAND

The other major New World contender for champagne's crown. New Zealand's ideal cool growing conditions result in sophisticated sparkling wines, helped, in the case of top producers like Montana (Deutz) and Cloudy Bay (Pelorus), by champenois know-how. ☆☆→☆☆☆☆

PROSECCO

A soft slightly sweet sparkling wine (though a bit drier than ASTI) made in the Veneto from the Prosecco grape variety. ☆

ROSE

A number of the regions which produce sparkling wine also produce a rosé version – **Cava Rosado** is an example. But the country that has really gone for sparkling rosé in a big way is Australia from its best-selling strawberry flavoured Angas Brut to the more champagne-like Green Point. ☆→☆☆☆

SAUMUR BRUT

A traditional method sparkling wine made predominantly from Chenin Blanc. At its best it can be a reasonable substitute for champagne, though it can be rather acidic. ☆☆

SEKT

Sekt is the German word for sparkling wine, although much of the wine that goes into the large commercial brands is produced outside Germany itself. (If the grapes do originate in Germany it will be labelled Deutscher Sekt and is likely to be of better quality.) "Trocken" is the indication that it it is dry – and it can in fact be quite sharp. Halbtrocken (literally "half dry") versions also exist. ☆

SHIRAZ & OTHER SPARKLING REDS

Australia is in the vanguard of red sparkling wine production with exuberantly fruity wines like Sparkling Shiraz, **Sparkling Cabernet** and **Sparkling Grenache** that are perfect for barbecues and summer eating (and are,

curiously, a brilliant match for chocolate desserts). By and large this is not a style favoured in the Old World with the notable exception of **Lambrusco**, the authentic version of which is refreshingly tart. A few red sparkling wines are also made in the Loire. ☆☆→☆☆☆

VEUVE DU VERNAY

Rather dull commercial French sparkler which has been overtaken in the quality and value-for-money stakes by its competitors. ☆☆

VOUVRAY MOUSSEUX

A softly honeyed, sparkling version of Vouvray generally a cut above the other Chenin Blanc sparklers of the Loire. If you want a dry wine, make sure it isn't a one of the elegant Demi-Sec versions also available. ☆☆→☆☆☆

Storing and serving

It is not worth laying down New World or non vintage champagne for any length of time, although most champagnes can benefit from a six month rest before you pop the cork. Vintage champagnes will last a good deal longer: from three to five years for basic vintage champagnes (depending, of course, on how long they've been stored by the time you buy them), to a good decade in the case of prestige cuvées. A bigger bottle will last longer than a smaller one. It is important to chill champagne well before serving – it not only tastes better, it makes it safer to open the bottle.

SWEET WINES

It is a shame that sweet wines have become such a marginal taste as they represent some of the most luscious and complex flavours in the wine world. However, the combination of their sheer sweetness and alcoholic strength undoubtedly makes them special occasion rather than everyday drinking.

Historically, sweet wines were more highly regarded than dry. The wine drunk by the Greeks and the Romans was intensely sweet, often infused with herbs or spices. In a hot climate it was the only kind of wine stable enough to survive. The effect of noble rot (the fungus that causes grapes to shrivel, concentrating their juice to a wonderful intensity) was probably recognised as far back as Roman times and certainly in the 17th century, when the great Hungarian wine Tokay was first produced.

Noble rot

Traditionally, the great areas for dessert wines have been where noble rot is readily cultivated: Bordeaux and the Loire Valley in France, and parts of Germany, Austria and Hungary. The rot or "botrytis" thrives on certain autumnal weather conditions – cool misty mornings and warm afternoons. This high risk strategy of leaving the grapes on the vine long enough to be affected by botrytis, then painstakingly harvesting the affected berries helps to explain the stratospheric prices of wines like Sauternes. But the wonderfully liquorous texture and uniquely rich, honeyed flavour of these wines is a benchmark for all dessert wines.

There are other methods of making sweet wines. Grapes may be hung up or laid out to dry – as favoured in Greece, France and Italy; the wine's eventual strength and concentration depends on how dessicated they get. Another method, popular for Muscat (*see* entry), is to add alcohol before the fermentation process is complete, creating a strong, sweet wine which retains its floral, aromatic character; this type of wine is called *vin doux naturel*. Some wines are made dry, and have sweet grape juice added, while others have their sweetness boosted with sugar.

Muscat, with its aromatic, floral character, is the grape variety most associated with dessert wines, but other light skinned grape varieties are also used extensively. The two stars are Riesling and Sémillon, both particularly susceptible to noble rot, but some fine wines are also made from Chenin (in the Loire) and Gewürztraminer (Alsace).

With so many different styles, sweet wines are confusing, but the easiest way to get a grip on them is by colour and price. The lighter the colour, the lighter the style. A pale straw coloured wine will taste lighter and fresher than a rich apricot coloured one. (The colour of these wines deepens over time: a darker colour may also indicate an older wine.)

Inexpensive wines, including most Muscats, tend to be less sweet than more expensively produced botrytised wines like Sauternes or intensely concentrated wines like Eiswein or Trockenbeerenauslese which are so sweet they can only sipped in tiny amounts. Check the sweetness rating (1–5) alongside each entry.

Many more expensive dessert wines need ageing to counterbalance their initial sweetness. German Rieslings in particular can be unbearably sweet to begin with, only starting to show a graceful balance after several years in the bottle. Chenin – the basis of the famous Loire dessert wines like Vouvray and Bonnezeaux can go through a "dumb" period, when they really are quite dull, before emerging in all their honeyed majesty. Like aged reds, the taste of mature sweets wine may not immediately appeal, but they are worth persevering with.

The big advantage of dessert wines is that you can buy most of them in half bottles. And for a dinner party that's all you need to give your guests a really rather special treat.

Label Clues

Look out for words that indicate the wine is sweet: Botrytis or Botrytised, Late Harvest, Late Picked, Vendange Tardive, Moelleux, Liquoreux, Doux and Dulce. Alcohol content is slightly less important than it is for other wines. A southern French Muscat of 15 degrees for instance may not taste as sweet as a German Beerenauslese of seven or eight degrees.

Starting points	
Light	**Rich**
Moscatel de Valencia	Muscat de Beaumes de Venise
Premières Côtes de Bordeaux	Late Harvest Riesling or Sémillon
Coteaux du Layon	Tokay
Sauternes	Vin Santo
Intensely sweet	**Sweet Red Wines**
Beerenauslese	Mavrodaphne of Patras
Trockenbeerenauslese	South African Muscadel
Eiswein	Recioto della Valpolicella

Above *Grapes affected by the revolting looking rot called "botrytis" (or noble rot) produce the most luscious, honeyed wines that can age for decades.*

Far left *Warm autumn mists rising from the Ciron stream running through Sauternes and Barsac encourage the growth of "botrytis" which makes these wines so special.*

AUSBRUCH

An Austrian wine classification indicating an intensely concentrated sweet wine made from BOTRYTIS-affected grapes – an Austrian equivalent to SAUTERNES if you like. Most is produced around the town of Rust. ☆☆

AUSLESE

Auslese is the recognised German wine category for grapes that are selected for being particularly ripe. It is generally sweet (though there are some dry versions) but not as sweet as BEERENAUSLESE. Quality varies considerably from the slightly sickly, commercial Auslesen, to very fine, concentrated, elegant RIESLINGS from individual growers. A similar classification is used in Austria. ☆→☆☆☆

BARSAC

The name of the most celebrated individual village in SAUTERNES which has its own appellation but may call its wines Barsac-Sauternes. The wines are virtually indistinguishable from those of Sauternes and the appellation includes many of Bordeaux's best properties, most notably **Château Climens**. ☆☆→☆☆☆

BEERENAUSLESE

The next grade of sweetness up from AUSLESE involving even riper grapes, usually those affected by BOTRYTIS. The resulting wine is intensely sweet, though generally balanced by a high level of acidity. ☆☆→☆☆☆

BONNEZEAUX

One of the two great sweet wines of the Loire from the COTEAUX DU LAYON area, the other being **Quarts de Chaume**. These are made from Chenin Blanc and are not at their best for at least 10 years and may last at least a couple of decades longer than that. ☆☆☆

BOTRYTIS/BOTRYTISED

A description used on labels to indicate that the wine is made from grapes affected by noble rot (*see* previous pages). In the New World this is quite likely to have been induced artifically. ☆☆→☆☆☆

COTEAUX DE L'AUBANCE

One of the best-kept secrets of the Loire – a small appellation just to the north of COTEAUX DU LAYON producing fine elegant Chenin-based wines. Rare. ☆☆→☆☆☆

COTEAUX DU LAYON

A large appellation in Anjou in the Loire Valley producing a wide range of wines from Chenin, from simple honeyed, medium-dry whites, to richer, complex wines from individual villages such as **Chaume** and **Rablay**. ☆☆→☆☆☆

EISWEIN

The most intensely sweet of all dessert wines made from frozen grapes which are picked as late as January. It is a particular speciality of Northern Germany, though there is also some made in Austria, and it is increasingly popular in Canada and Washington State where is is called **Icewine**. Because of the very low yields – and its fashionability, particularly among Far Eastern buyers – it commands very high prices. ☆☆☆

GEWURZTRAMINER

A grape variety well suited to dessert wine production, particularly in Alsace which has established a reputation for powerful, rich, aromatic VENDANGE TARDIVE and SELECTION DES GRAINS NOBLES wines. They can lose their distinctive aromatic quality over time. ☆☆☆

GRAVES SUPERIEURES

A less well-known Bordeaux appellation that can produce some decent basic sweet wines, but which only hint at the opulence of neighbouring SAUTERNES and BARSAC. ☆

JURANCON MOELLEUX

A fine, elegantly honeyed dessert wine from the southwest of France, near the Spanish border, made from local grape varieties, principally Petit Manseng. ☆☆→☆☆☆

LATE HARVEST/LATE PICKED

The anglicized version of VENDANGE TARDIVE: a term used predominantly in the New World to indicate a sweet wine made from super-ripe grapes. ☆→☆☆

MAVRODAPHNE OF PATRAS

An exotic, rich, almost port-like red Greek dessert wine that is one of the best inexpensive wine matches for chocolate. ☆

MONBAZILLAC

A sweet SEMILLON/Sauvignon-based wine from the Bergerac region in the southwest of France made in a similar style, though not always attaining the same quality, as sweet Bordeaux. The best examples, however, can be real bargains. ☆ ☆

MONTLOUIS

A neighbouring appellation to VOUVRAY, but much less well-known. Montlouis wines have a similar honeyed style, but not are always as distinguished. A limited amount of botrytised dessert wine is also produced in exceptional years in nearby appellation of **Jasnières**. ☆ ☆ ☆

MOSCATEL DE VALENCIA

A light, refreshingly grapey Spanish MUSCAT that represents exceptionally good value for money. It frequently comes in a distinctive frosted flute-shaped bottle. ☆

MOSCATO PASSITO DI PANTELLERIA

An intense rich golden, almost apricot-like MUSCAT, from the island of Pantelleria off Sicily, made by the *passito* method from grapes laid out to dry until they resemble raisins. ☆ ☆

MUSCADEL

A dark berried South African strain of MUSCAT, traditionally used for the famous South African fortified wine **Constantia**, but also used to make a rich, sweet port-like dessert wine. ☆

MUSCAT, MOSCATO, MOSCATEL

The Muscat grape is used all over the wine world to make an astonishingly diverse range of wines, from the fresh, grapey **Moscatel de Valencia**, to the intensely rich, toffeed **Liqueur Muscats** of the Rutherglen region in Australia. Confusingly, there are more than 200 different varieties of Muscat, but the most widely planted are Muscat Blanc à Petits Grains and Muscat d'Alexandrie which go under a number of different synonyms. Most are in fact a **vin doux naturel** (*see* pages 92–93). Although this technically brings them into the fortified category, most Muscats are regarded primarily as a dessert wine, rather than one to sip at the end of a meal like port. In fact, Muscats, like those from Frontignan and Beaumes de Venise (*see* below), are frequently served as an aperitif in France. Richer, heavier styles like Australian Liqueur Muscats are dealt with in the next section and sparkling wines made from Muscat (Moscato) on page 90. ☆ → ☆ ☆ ☆

MUSCAT D'ALSACE

Muscat is usually produced as a dry wine in Alsace but some winemakers do produce VENDANGE TARDIVE (late picked) versions which are usually both elegant and expensive. ☆ ☆ ☆

Food and occasions

While sweet wines are the obvious choice to accompany a dessert, you can also drink them, as the French do, as an aperitif. The general rule with a dessert is that the wine should be sweeter than the pudding. Lighter wines such as Muscats and sweet Bordeaux are best with simple fruit flavours, particularly apple-, pear- or peach-based desserts (red fruits can be tricky unless they are offset by cream). For richer puddings, such as those made from chocolate, look to more robust wines such as Australian liqueur Muscats or even sweet red wines.

MUSCAT DE BEAUMES-DE-VENISE

Less fashionable than it once was but still one of the very best-known Muscats on the market, this luscious sweet wine from the southern end of the Rhône Valley is one of the easiest ways into dessert wine drinking. ☆☆

MUSCAT DE FRONTIGNAN

Originally the most important of the southern French Muscats that are produced in the Languedoc, Frontignan – as it is now called – is made in a much lighter style than than the dark, rich, raisiny wines that used to predominate in the region. Other similarly styled Languedoc Muscats are **Muscat de Lunel**, **Muscat de Miréval**, **Muscat de Rivesaltes** and **Muscat St-Jean-de-Minervois**. ☆

ORANGE MUSCAT

A characteristic style of MUSCAT that has been enterprisingly promoted by Andrew Quady in Calfornia and Brown Brothers in Australia: rich and liquorous with a pronounced orange-peel aroma and flavour. ☆☆

PACHERENC DU VIC-BILH – Moelleux

A rare but highly regarded dessert wine produced in the foothills of the Pyrénées in southwest France. Pacherenc du Vic-Bilh is made in a similar style to JURANCON which comes from nearby. ☆☆ → ☆☆☆

PREMIERES COTES DU BORDEAUX

A large area on the right bank of the Garonne which now produces more dry white, rosé and red wines than it does dessert wines. Basic sweet Premières Côtes du Bordeaux is rarely distinguished, but some fine SAUTERNES-type wines are produced in individual villages such as **Cadillac** and the better-known **Loupiac** and **Ste-Croix-du-Mont**. ☆☆

RECIOTO DELLA VALPOLICELLA

This obscure sweet red dessert wine is made from the same grape varieties as Valpolicella (*see* page 65), but left out to dry for several months on straw mats. **Recioto di Soave**, which is rarer still, is made in a similar fashion, though from light skinned grapes. ☆☆

RIESLING

Riesling is the grape variety used in Germany's finest dessert wines, its high acidity proving a perfect counterfoil to what can be quite intense levels of sweetness. It is also a popular choice in Alsace and Austria and in the New World, particularly Australia, where it is widely used to make BOTRYTISED or LATE HARVEST wines. ☆☆ → ☆☆☆

SAUTERNES

One of the few areas to have the ideal conditions for the cultivation of noble rot, Sauternes wines are justly regarded as some of the finest in the world. Made principally from SEMILLON with a small amount of

Sauvignon and Muscadelle, when young it has a light, luscious honey and citrus character which ages gracefully over time to a richer, nuttier flavour of dried apricots, figs and toasted hazelnuts. Higher quality wines are named after the five major villages in the region, the most famous of which is BARSAC. The most celebrated individual property is **Château d'Yquem**, whose better vintages can last for more than a century. ☆☆☆ → ☆☆☆☆

SELECTION DES GRAINS NOBLES

The sweetest and most expensive of Alsace wines achieved by hand-selecting ultra ripe, often BOTRYTISED grapes from MUSCAT, Pinot Gris, RIESLING or GEWURZTRAMINER vines. ☆☆☆

SEMILLON

The backbone of SAUTERNES and the other sweet wines of Bordeaux and Bergerac, the Sémillon grape's thin skin makes it ideal for sweet wine-making because of its susceptibility to noble rot. It is also widely used in Australia to make LATE HARVEST and BOTRYTISED wines. ☆☆

TOKAY

Tokay, or Tokaji as it is called in Hungary, is undoubtedly one of the world's great classic dessert wines, having been produced there for over three centuries. The most widely available style is **Tokay Aszú**, a sumptuously rich, golden wine brimming with luscious dried fig, raisin and apricot flavours. It is officially graded by the number of "puttonyos" it contains (barrels of sweet grape pulp that are added to the wine before the secondary fermentation, three "putts" being the least sweet and six the sweetest). The rarest kind of Tokay is **Essencia** which is made from the minute amounts of juice that ooze out of the BOTRYTISED grapes. Tokay remains an extraordinary bargain. ☆☆

TROCKENBEERENAUSLESE

Trockenbeerenauslese (or TBA as it is known for short) is principally a German dessert wine that is made only in exceptional years from hand-picked BOTRYTISED grapes. The result is an intensely liquorous sweet wine but with a piercing acidity which prevents it from being cloying. In fact the ideal conditions for making TBA occur more readily in the Burgenland region of Austria which is able to supply them at a more reasonable price. Indeed innovative Austrian producer Willi Opitz makes a red TBA. ☆☆☆

VENDANGE TARDIVE

A term used principally in Alsace to indicate that a wine has been made from LATE PICKED grapes. It is normally an indication of sweetness. ☆☆→☆☆☆

VIN DE PAILLE

A rare speciality of the Jura region of France made from grapes that are laid out to dry on straw mats (pailles). The resulting wine

is intensely sweet and almost sherried. "Straw wine" is also made in Germany where it is called **Strohwein** and Austria (**Schilfwein**), though these tend to be rather lighter in style. ☆☆☆

VIN SANTO

Over the past few years Vin Santo, along with other Tuscan wines, has become extremely fashionable and consequently expensive. Made from grapes that are either hung or laid out to dry then aged in barrels for anything up to six to eight years, it produces a glorious, golden, nutty wine, which is traditionally served at the end of meal with dipping biscuits (cantuccini). It is also made in Umbria and the Trentino. ☆☆→☆☆☆

VOUVRAY MOELLEUX

As well as producing dry and medium-dry (demi-sec) wines, Vouvray, which is made from Chenin Blanc, also produces some of the finest sweet wines in the Loire. They are labelled Moelleux or, in the case of the very sweetest, **Liquoreux**. Sweet and honeyed when young, they can still taste extraordinarily fresh and fruity after several decades. ☆☆→☆☆☆

Storing and serving

Most inexpensive dessert wines, particularly Muscats, benefit from being drunk quite young so that you get the full benefit of their fresh, grapey flavour. But many dessert wines particularly those from Bordeaux and the Loire have the capacity to age for much longer. Most dessert wines benefit from being well chilled – serve them in small rather than full-sized wine glasses. Once opened they will keep fresh for much longer than dry wines, certainly for a week, and in the case of Tokay or Vin Santo, for a good month or more.

SHERRY

Sherry, port and Madeira are not nearly as popular as they once were. With many more people regularly drinking wine, consumers prefer less alcoholic and less challenging drinks. Nevertheless, they remain some of the finest wines the world has to offer and their price scarcely reflects the care, time and effort that goes into their production.

The process of fortifying wine basically means adding alcohol in the form of spirit to a still wine, either to boost the alcoholic strength of a dry wine like sherry, or to arrest the fermentation of a wine like port or Muscat to achieve a sweeter style. Originally it was a purely functional device to enable the wine to last longer – now it is more a question of enabling the winemaker to achieve the style of wine he's looking for.

Most wines are fortified to 17 to 18 degrees, though fino sherry can be lighter and vintage port and other rich fortified wines more alcoholic.

Spanish style sherry

The sherry Spain produces for export is very different to the sherry the Spanish drink themselves. The world sees it as a rather sweet, sticky, fortified wine. The real thing is deliciously tangy and in the main bone dry and well worth getting to know.

Sherry can only be made in a tiny triangle of southern Spain bordered by the towns of Sanlúcar de Barrameda, Puerto de Santa María and Jerez de la Frontera – the town sherry is named after. Its intensely hot, dry climate and distinctive chalky soil is ideally suited for the production of this uniquely dry, yet full-flavoured style of wine.

The two main types of sherry are fino and oloroso – both made from the local Palomino grape, but subsequently treated very differently. Fino, the lighter style, is fortified to about 15 degrees, then transferred to oak barrels where it develops and then matures under a thick layer of yeast called *flor*. It is the flor that gives the distinctive pale colour and dry, tangy character. Oloroso is fortified to a higher 18 degrees, too strong for flor to develop, and makes a much richer, darker wine.

What gives sherry its distinctive character is the *solera* system, in which wine of differing vintages is kept in rows of barrels, stacked one on top of the other. As the wine from the lower barrels is drawn off for bottling, it is topped up with younger wine from the barrels above, ensuring there is always a freshness to the wine to match its depth and complexity. In the case of fino, the final wine is then fortified again to between 15 and 17 degrees. The whole process can take at least four or five years (to be called sherry it has to be matured for at least three).

Light and dry
FINO

A very light, crisp, dry style of sherry which gets its characteristically tangy taste from the thick layer of yeast (*flor*) under which the wine ages. The Spanish version will be bone dry – piercingly so in the case of a wine like Tio Pepe. Finos produced purely for the export market tend to be smoother and sweeter. ☆→☆☆

MANZANILLA

Generally even drier than FINO, manzanilla is produced in the coastal town of Sanlúcar which gives it its characteristic, almost salty tang. ☆☆

Light and sweet
PALE CREAM SHERRY

A light, smooth, FINO sherry, sweetened to satisfy the tastes of the export market. ☆

Rich and dry
AMONTILLADO SECO

This is, in fact, FINO sherry, matured beyond the flor stage until it develops a dark golden colour and a delicious dry, nutty, toffee flavour. ☆☆→☆☆☆

OLOROSO SECO

Darker and more intense than AMONTILLADO with a rich, raisiny, figgy flavour. ☆☆→☆☆☆

PALO CORTADO

Another authentic Spanish style sherry, slightly richer in style than a dry AMONTILLADO, but not quite as rich and concentrated as an OLOROSO. ☆☆→☆☆☆

Rich and sweet
MEDIUM DRY AMONTILLADO

Although described as "medium dry" by Spanish standards, this style of wine is quite sweet. ☆

OLOROSO DULCE

Sweet oloroso is one of most glorious after-dinner wines around: a dark, sumptuously sweet wine, almost like liquid Christmas pudding. ☆☆→☆☆☆

RICH CREAM SHERRY

The British style version of an OLOROSO DULCE: equally sweet but without the balancing depth of flavour. ☆

PEDRO XIMENEZ

An extraordinarily intense, dark, treacly sherry used to make OLOROSO DULCE but also bottled on its own. Almost too sweet to drink, it makes a sensational topping for vanilla ice-cream. ☆☆

MONTILLA and other sherry-style wines

A number of wines are made in a similar style to sherry including Montilla and other fortified wines from Britain, Cyprus and South Africa – few of which have sherry's distinction. Exceptions are **Cape White Jerepigo**, a South African wine similar to a dry AMONTILLADO and the FINO-like **Vin Jaune** which comes from the Jura region of France. ☆→☆☆☆

Food and occasions

Do not be embarrassed to serve up sherry: it's not at all a stuffy drink! Fino or dry amontillado makes a perfect aperitif. Fino is the classic partner for Spanish tapas and goes well with spicy food, seafood or fish. It is also the traditional match for soup. Richer sherries like dry and sweet oloroso are a good alternative to port with cheese or as an after-dinner drink.

Storing and serving

Fino and manzanilla should be served chilled and as fresh as possible (within 48 hours of opening the bottle). Other sherries should be served at room temperature, but should still be consumed within a few weeks of opening. Neither type of sherry should be decanted. If you drink sherry regularly it's worth investing in a set of Spanish style copita glasses rather than the traditional schooner which tends to subdue the flavours and aromas of the wine.

PORT

Sweet, spicy port is one of the most comforting drinks in the world: a classic end to a Christmas meal, a warming winter nightcap or even the kind of drink to sip as you curl up with a good book.

First made in Portugal in the eighteenth century in response to the demand for a wine that could survive the journey back to England, much about port is still deeply traditional. The vertiginous slopes of the Douro River Valley which are still almost totally resistant to any kind of mechanisation, the fact that grapes are still trodden by foot, the whole arcane ritual of serving that still lingers on in gentleman's clubs and regimental dinners are all legacies of a bygone age. Even the names of the port houses, Cockburn's, Graham's, Taylor's, Warre's, reflect the enduring British interest in the area.

Port is made from a wide variety of indigenous Portuguese grapes of which the most widely used are Touriga Nacional, Touriga Francesca, Tinta Barroca, Tinta Cao and Tinta Roriz. The basic process is simply a question of adding brandy to the partially fermented wine, leaving it with a high degree of sweetness. It is then aged in oak casks for several years before it is either blended with other older or younger wines or bottled as a port from a single vintage. Ports of exceptional quality are bottled early and left to mature in bottle, a slower and more gradual process than ageing them in cask.

The most obvious difference in style is between ruby and tawny port and it's very much a question of personal taste as to whether you like the warming, winter punch-type taste of a Late Bottled Vintage or the drier, nuttier more sherry-like taste of a tawny.

Equally significant is the age of the port – and port is a drink that lasts a very long time. There's more of a difference between a young, fresh, ruby port and a mature vintage port than there is between a basic ruby and a tawny. You may in fact prefer the taste of the younger wine.

Port-style wines

Australia is the country that ostensibly models its fortified wines most closely on port, marketing them as Tawny or Aged Tawny but, in fact, they are sweeter and a lot more fudgy than authentic aged tawny ports – more like an Australian Liqueur Muscat. Some port-style fortified wines are also produced in California and South Africa but the wines that are most similar in taste to port are the fortified wines of the Roussillon: Banyuls, Maury and Rivesaltes (*see* Madeira and other fortified wines).

RUBY PORT

A blend of different wines bottled after two to three years' storage in cask, concrete or even stainless steel. Simple, sweet and brambly. ☆

VINTAGE CHARACTER

Easy to confuse with vintage port but in fact only a marginal step up in quality from basic RUBY PORT. ☆

LATE BOTTLED VINTAGE (LBV)

Late Bottled Vintage is port from a single vintage that has been matured in cask for four to six years. Generally it is then released for immediate drinking, though some producers mature their wines further in the bottle like a VINTAGE PORT. LBV is much richer and more complex than basic RUBY PORT, with a warming spiciness. ☆ ☆

VINTAGE PORT

Port producers do not "declare", a vintage every year, only in what they consider to be an exceptional harvest or when they haven't declared one for a while. Unlike other ports, vintage ports are bottled after two years and sold immediately, but are then intended to carry on maturing in the bottle for at least another 10–20 years, during which time they accumulate a heavy sediment. The resulting wine is richly flavoured, complex and mellow with deep plum, raisin and chocolate flavours. ☆ ☆ ☆

CRUSTED PORT

Similar to a VINTAGE PORT, but the produce of more than one year. It is bottled a little later, then allowed to mature for a further three or four years in the bottle. This makes for a slightly lighter style of wine. ☆ ☆

TAWNY PORT

Basic tawny port is generally made from inferior quality wine to ruby port, blended with WHITE PORT to give it its distinctive pale colour. It has little of the depth or nutty character of an aged tawny port. ☆

10-YEAR-OLD TAWNY

The most popular style of tawny has a rich, nutty, toffeed character that comes from an average of ten years' cask ageing. ☆ ☆

20, 30 AND 40-YEAR-OLD TAWNIES

As TAWNY PORTS age, they develop a rich, creamy, nutty, intensely elegant style. Thirty and 40-year-old tawnies are very rare and have a particularly pronounced toasty, nutty character, verging towards complete dryness. ☆ ☆ ☆

COLHEITA

This is a TAWNY PORT from a single vintage which has been matured for at least seven years in cask. A rather more individual and characterful style of port than the standard 10-YEAR-OLD TAWNY. ☆ ☆

SINGLE QUINTA

A high quality port made on a single estate or *quinta* in years when there isn't a vintage declaration. It is released after about 10 years and is a little lighter than VINTAGE PORT but significantly cheaper. ☆ ☆

WHITE PORT

Widely drunk in Portugal as a summer drink with tonic, most white port is made in medium-dry style, similar to a pale cream sherry, though there are drier versions that have a crisper, nuttier flavour. ☆

Food and occasions

Too often port is served at the end of an already long and heavy meal, but it makes a better accompaniment to a small snack like cheese and crackers or a piece of cake. Aged tawny ports can make a stylish aperitif.

Storing and serving

It is a myth that all ports need to be decanted. The ones that do are those that accumulate a heavy sediment like vintage port, crusted ports and single quinta ports. The other myth about port is that once opened it will keep indefinitely. In fact, you should drink it within a month. The big danger, with vintage port in particular, is opening it up before it's ready. You shouldn't even think about it until it is at least 10 years old. Although most port is best served at room temperature, tawny port can be delicious lightly chilled.

MADEIRA AND OTHER FORTIFIED WINES

Though treated as a bit of a music hall joke, Madeira is undoubtedly up among the greats of the fortified wine world. Its finest wines have the capacity to last not only for decades, but for centuries.

This style of wine developed accidentally as a result of heating up during long voyages across the equator. These days a similar effect is achieved by warming up the wine in large concrete tanks or in a heated room (both called an *estufa*), though better quality Madeira is aged more slowly in oak casks at a temperature of about 25°C. (Some wines involve a combination of the two methods.)

Madeira is made in four principle styles named after the grape varieties they are made from, the common characteristic is high acidity. **Sercial** is the driest – light, tangy and crisp with a faint, honeyed flavour offset by a characteristic acidity. It is generally fuller in flavour than a fino sherry, though it develops a drier, more almondy flavour with age. Like fino it can be drunk lightly chilled as an aperitif. **Verdelho** is fuller-flavoured and nuttier, more like an amontillado sherry. It can also be made in a medium-bodied, but slightly lighter, less dry style.

Bual is distinctly sweet, but full-bodied, nutty and raisiny with a fragrant, almost smoky character. It can be a good with cheese instead of a tawny port. **Malmsey** is the sweetest of the Madeira styles and is in fact made from the Malvasia grape variety, whose name got corrupted to Malmsey. It is intensely rich with a dark treacle-toffee colour and flavour, like a sticky and well matured fruit cake, but because of its high level of acidity it isn't remotely cloying. It makes an exotic finale to a special dinner.

A significant amount of Madeira is not made from these grapes but the more widely planted Tinta Negra Mole variety. These are bottled either as basic Madeira (labelled "dry", "medium dry", "sweet" or, somewhat misleadingly, "Finest") or under English-sounding names such as "Duke of Clarence".

Madeira's age is timed from the completion of the *estufagem* (the heating process). The basic styles are released after three years, Reserves after five years, Special Reserves after 10, and vintage wines only after 20 years in cask and two further years in bottle, though they will easily last another 20–40 years (a fact reflected in their rarity and price). There are also "Solera Madeiras" which carry the date when the ageing process was first established, such as "Solera 1900". (These shouldn't be confused with vintage Madeiras which are made only from grapes harvested in that year.)

AUSTRALIAN LIQUEUR MUSCAT

Aptly called a "sticky", this highly individual style of dark, sweet, syrupy Muscat with its sumptuously rich, treacle-toffee flavour is a speciality of the Rutherglen region in Victoria. ☆☆

BANYULS, MAURY AND RIVESALTES

A trio of fortified wines from the Roussillon region in southern France made predominantly from Grenache. When young they tend to be rich, raisiny and porty. Older versions are often made in what is called a *rancio* style. This indicates a high degree of oxidation giving the wine a sharper, slightly nuttier character that is rather more of an acquired taste. ☆☆

MALAGA

Although Málaga, like sherry, covers a range of styles, it is most often associated with the intensely sweet, dark, raisiny wine called **Dulce**. Made in Andalucia in southern Spain, it is produced mainly from Pedro Ximénez (the same grape variety that makes the sweetest type of sherry) together with a little Moscatel. It is not strictly a fortified wine but made by a curious amalgam of techniques: part fortified, partly from dried grapes that are fermented and partly from a boiled dark, treacly concentrate of grape juice. It must be aged in oak for at least two years before release which is carried out in a *solera*-type system (*see* pages 98–99). ☆→☆☆

MARSALA

A Sicilian fortified wine better known for its role in cooking than as a dessert or aperitif wine. As with MALAGA there is a range of styles, though it is the darker, sweeter versions that one encounters most often. The wine is produced from local Grillo and Catarrato grapes fortified to at least 17 degrees (supplemented by concentrated grape juice) and aged for upwards of a year in oak casks. The basic quality is called Fine while Superiore must have an alcohol content of 18 degrees and have been aged for at least two years (four in the case of a Superiore Riserva). Wines are also labelled by colour – Ambra (amber), Oro (gold) and Rubino (ruby) and by the degree of sweetness – Secco (dry), Semisecco (medium-dry) and Dolce (sweet). The most highly regarded Marsala however is **Vergine**, a fine, dry, elegantly nutty wine which has to be aged for at least five years. ☆☆

RASTEAU

The name both of a village in the Côtes du Rhône region and of a rich, spicy, plummy, fortified wine very similar in style to those from Roussillon – BANYULS, MAURY AND RIVESALTES. ☆☆

SETUBAL and other full-bodied Moscatels and Muscats

Fuller-bodied, often dark, treacly Moscatels such as Setúbal are popular for local consumption throughout Spain and Portugal (*see* also MALAGA), though not much gets exported. Greece also produces some fine, rich Muscats such as **Muscat de Lemnos**, **Samos Vin Doux Naturel** and **Visanto** from the island of Santorini. ☆→☆☆

Storing and serving

Served in similar ways to other fortified wines – drier wines as aperitifs and sweeter ones at the end of the meal. Madeira has the rare distinction of keeping almost indefinitely once the bottle is open. Also useful to have to hand in the kitchen is Marsala which is traditionally used for making zabaglione.

WINE AND FOOD

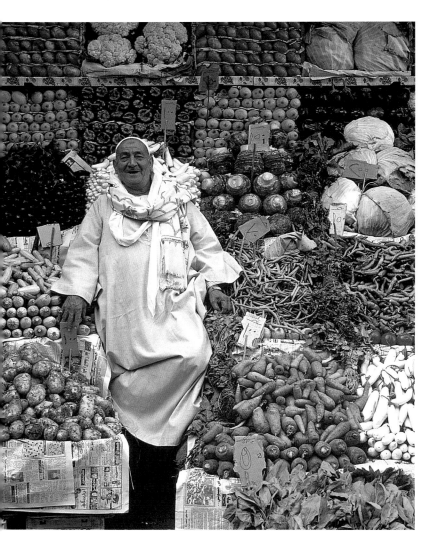

Just as wine has changed, so has food. The fairly narrow spectrum of dishes we enjoyed in the past has blossomed into a heady cornucopia of ingredients and flavours. Although in parts of France and Italy people still eat the same kind of food as their parents did, in countries with a less strong cooking tradition like Britain, Australia or the United States, we now borrow ideas and techniques from every corner of the globe.

The effect of this revolution is that a lot of traditional so-called rules about matching food and wine have become irrelevant. At one time the idea that you shouldn't drink red wine with fish made sense. Plainly cooked white fish didn't (and doesn't) go with an astringent tannic red. But season it with a spicy marinade, barbecue it and serve it with a soft fruity New World Pinot Noir and it's sensational.

The truth is that it's misleading to make hard and fast rules. Even if you say that a particular dish normally goes with a particular style of wine it will in the end depend on how that dish is cooked, whether the wine is typical of its kind and – most importantly – whether you yourself actually like that combination of flavours.

This isn't to argue that it's not worth trying to find a wine that will go reasonably well with what you're eating, more to say that you shouldn't worry too much about finding the perfect match. There are few really dire combinations and a quick check through the points below should help you avoid most of them.

Order of serving The white before red rule may no longer be appropriate, but in most meals it still makes sense to serve drier wines before sweeter ones, younger wines before older vintages, and lighter-bodied before fuller-bodied ones.

Intensity of flavour More useful than the "red wine with meat, white wine with fish" rule is to think about the weight and intensity of flavour of the dish you're serving or ordering. If it's a full-flavoured dish it will call for a full-bodied wine (which may well be red). If it's a lighter one, it will need a lighter wine. That may come down primarily to the cooking method (or absence of it). Raw, steamed or poached food tend to call for lighter wines. Roast and chargrilled dishes for more robust ones.

Which flavours are dominant? Frequently the seasoning which is used in a dish or the sauce in which it is cooked has more effect on the final flavour than the main ingredient. It is more helpful to concentrate on what wines go with, say a Mediterranean style tomato and garlic flavoured sauce or a Thai style stir-fry than to ask yourself which wines go with chicken or pork.

Complement or contrast? You can go for two effects when you choose a wine. Either you can complement the texture and flavour of the dish you're making or you can look for a contrast.

For example, if you were serving a chicken dish with a rich, creamy mushroom sauce you could either go for a smooth, dry white like a Chardonnay with a similarly creamy texture or for an aromatic white like a Riesling which would provide a more exotic note.

If you're unsure what to do just think of it in cooking terms. A crisp, citrussy white will have the same effect on a piece of grilled or fried fish as a squeeze of lemon. If it's a meat dish that requires some sweetness, then serve it with a fruity New World red. If you want to cut the rich, slightly fatty taste of cold roast pork then try a crisp appley white or a fresh juicy Beaujolais.

Food-friendly wines If you're eating out in a restaurant, you'll often have to choose a bottle that will suit what several people have ordered. And even if you're eating at home, a selection of dishes could be on the table at the same time. What you need is a wine that will go with the maximum number of flavours and offend the least number of people.

My own choices would be a lightly oaked or unoaked Chardonnay, a crisp Sauvignon, a New World Pinot Noir or Merlot or a crisp dry rosé. In a restaurant I didn't know, those would tend to be from the New World.

Tried and tested combinations Although it is fun to experiment, do not overlook the conventional options entirely – particularly when it comes to French and Italian food. Most stand the test of time. In a restaurant in a wine producing area I would always go for the local wine. It will be better value and more likely to suit the style of cooking.

Finally, a word or two to explain the rest of this section. Over the page you'll find suggestions of wines to go with particular styles of cooking and following that there are suggestions of dishes to pair with different styles of wine. Don't regard these as definitive – you may well find that a wine I've suggested will go with one type of food may well go equally well with another. As in everything else to do with wine, the best way to find out is to experiment.

CLASSIC FRENCH

Drinking wine is a way of life in France, so it's no surprise that the food of each major wine region blends seamlessly with its wines. The spiciness of an Alsace Pinot Gris lifts the rich creaminess of a chicken in mushroom sauce; the crisp, acidity of a Muscadet is the ideal partner for the shellfish of the Loire region; the rich casseroles and braises of Burgundian cuisine not only benefit from being cooked in the local wine but taste good with it too. It makes perfect sense to follow the example of the French and drink the wine of the region.

MEDITERRANEAN

Although mainly associated with the south of France, the Mediterranean style of cooking extends right through southern Europe, encompassing the cooking of Spain, Portugal and southern Italy. Common to them all are the vivid flavours of tomatoes, peppers, garlic and olives, together with pungent herbs like basil, rosemary and oregano. Fish is more common than meat and frequently incorporated into robustly flavoured soups or stews like *bouillabaisse*. Dry, crisp white or rosé (*rosado*) wines often work better than red with this style of food though light fruity reds are ideal with pizza or *pissaladière*.

NORTHERN ITALY

What is thought of as Italian cooking is fundamentally the cooking of the north and centre of Italy, rather than the south. Nevertheless, even within these boundaries there are major differences between the seafood-based cooking of Venice, for example, and the heartier, more robust cooking of Piedmont. As in France, the local wines are often the best choice. Comparatively neutral, crisp Italian white wines work well with many Italian dishes such as seafood, creamy pasta, classic *risotto*, and *osso buco*. And the marked acidity of many Italian reds is a good foil to richer pasta dishes such as *lasagne*.

TRADITIONAL BRITISH & IRISH

The British have always had a taste for well-aged wine and, indeed, the plainly cooked roasts, pies and casseroles that are typical of traditional British and Irish cooking are highly complimentary to delicately flavoured fine wines like mature Rioja, claret and burgundy. Scotch and Irish salmon is as good as anywhere in the world: simply cooked it is the perfect foil for fine white burgundy, while smoked salmon is surprisingly successful with a wide range of wines including champagne, Sauvignon Blanc and drier English whites. Traditional English cheeses can be among the easiest to pair with fine wines. Port and stilton is the classic combination but can be heavy. Try the slightly lighter *vin doux naturels* from the south of France like Banyuls or Rivesaltes.

CENTRAL AND EAST EUROPEAN

Again the cooking of central Europe such as Germany, Austria and Hungary is relatively plain, but often involves some tricky matches for wine such as smoked meats and *sauerkraut*. Crisp, dry whites are generally a better solution than reds. Riesling is perfect with the local cuisine, especially pork or fish dishes with a creamy sauce. Austria and Hungary, with their love of paprika, have a slightly more robust style of cooking. Crisp, dry whites will cope, as do peppery reds like Austria's Blaufränkisch. And again, dry whites, especially Chasselas, are the answer for the many cooked cheese dishes of Switzerland.

SCANDINAVIAN

With its emphasis on pickled foods, Scandinavia is more beer and schnapps than natural wine territory. But dry Gemanic style whites work better than anything else. The famous Swedish dish *gravadlax* (cured salmon with a dill and mustard sauce) is easier to pair with wine than it sounds, and goes well with either a German Riesling or Demi-Sec Vouvray. Here there is also a fondness for serving meat with tart red fruit, like cranberries and lingonberries. This needs a fruity red with a touch of acidity to match such as a Beaujolais.

MIDDLE EASTERN/NORTH AFRICAN

The southern half of the Mediterranean – Greece, Turkey and the Lebanon – has a more robust palate of flavours including lemon, garlic and raw onion, and spices such as coriander and cumin. The typical style of eating is to put several dishes on the table at once which calls for an all purpose wine that will cope with a wide range of flavours – a crisp, dry white or a rosé works best. The grilled meats of the region suit light, fruity reds, while the more spicy *tagines* or couscous of Morocco call for a more vigorous, full-bodied red with a touch of sweetness like a Shiraz – or even a Moroccan or Algerian red.

INDIAN

The widely held belief that Indian food doesn't go with wine rests on the assumption that it is all searingly hot. In fact, it embraces a wide range of different styles from the mild kormas of the north to the much spicier dishes of the south. The problem is you often get dishes of varying degrees of heat in the same meal. You could replicate the refreshing quality of lager by serving a clean, crisp, dry, neutral white or rosé. Alternatively, try serving a much fruitier New World style of wine such as an unoaked Chardonnay or a jammy Cabernet or Shiraz.

SOUTHEAST ASIAN

Also hot, but less spicy than Indian food, its distinguishing flavours – lemongrass, galangal and fresh coriander are quite wine friendly. Try crisp, citrussy whites like Sauvignon Blanc (New Zealand's tend to be the best match). Drier Alsace whites like Pinot Blanc and Pinot Gris also work well, as do Sémillon, unoaked Chardonnay and Australian Rieslings.

CHINESE

As with India, people often think of Chinese food as just one style, but there are marked differences between the delicate, subtlety of Cantonese cuisine and the more fiery flavours of Szechuan cooking. The conventional match with the former are aromatic whites such as Riesling and Gewürztraminer, although Viognier would also work and a Blanc de Blancs champagne can be sensational. With the latter you might try a Sauvignon Blanc or a light, fruity red like a Beaujolais.

JAPANESE

One of the trickier cuisines to pair with wine – the Japanese traditionally drink sake. With raw fish dishes like *sushi* and *sashimi* you want an ultra-dry white like Muscadet or even an extra-brut champagne. With more spicy, savoury *teppanyaki* dishes or a *teriyaki* sauce, a fruity, but not too oaky red would be a better choice. Try a Loire red, a Beaujolais Cru or an Austrian Blaufränkisch. (N.B. Hot and sour Japanese pickles are particularly tough on wine – try to avoid them if you're drinking anything decent.)

PACIFIC RIM

This style of cooking – much favoured in Australia, New Zealand and along the West Coast of America – is heavily influenced by Southeast Asia. It therefore goes best with similar types of wine to those cuisines – vivid New world Sauvignons, Chardonnays and Rieslings. The use of chargrilling can add a smoky note which is best offset by a fruity red like a Pinot Noir or a lighter Shiraz or Merlot.

CAJUN, CENTRAL & SOUTH AMERICAN

This increasingly popular style of cooking is dominated by spicy chillies and big, gutsy flavours that need correspondingly powerful wines to complement them. These are the perfect dishes to show off lush, full-bodied reds like California Zinfandel, Chilean Cabernets or Merlots or Argentinian Syrah or Malbec. For whites, look to zesty Chilean or South African Sauvignon Blancs (a good match for *ceviche* or *guacamole*).

AFRO/CARIBBEAN

With hot, spicy dishes like jerk chicken, curry goat and pepperpot, this is again a flavourful style of cooking that needs correspondingly full-flavoured wines such as a tropical fruity Chardonnay or a rich, plummy Shiraz.

NEW WORLD/ECLECTIC CUISINE

This is the kind of contemporary cuisine you'll find in fashionable restaurants in every capital city of the world. It borrows from every culinary tradition – from Italian to Japanese and encompasses every type of flavour. The pick and mix nature of the menu can make it difficult to find a bottle to suit every dish: so take advantage of wines that are available by the glass (as many are in these restaurants). Lighter Chardonnays, Sauvignon Blancs and New World Pinot Noirs all go well with this style of food, but this cuisine is all about breaking rules, so don't be afraid to break wine rules too. Seared tuna, for example, is just as good with a light red wine as a white.

TRADITIONAL AMERICAN

Unlike French or Italian food, traditional American food didn't grow up side by side with wine and many Americans, particularly in the deep south, still wouldn't drink it at all. Homely dishes like fried chicken and meatloaf taste best with simple, light reds or smooth, creamy whites. A classic American barbecue with sweet, sticky ribs needs something a bit fuller-bodied – ideally an all-American Zinfandel. For a creamy fish chowder try a light Chardonnay.

CRISP, FRESH, DRY WHITES

General Summery food – salads and steamed, grilled or barbecued fish. Mediterranean fish soups and stews. Fish and chips. Light stir fries, noodle dishes, mild curries.

Chablis (unoaked) Oysters, seafood, shellfish

Muscadet *Moules Marinières*, *plateau de fruits de mer*, oysters.

Sauvignon Blanc Seafood and shellfish. Asparagus. Grilled vegetables. Sancerre and other Loire Sauvignons: particularly good with goat's cheese. New World Sauvignon: dishes flavoured with garlic, ginger and coriander.

Soave, Frascati and other Italian whites *Antipasti*. Light pastas with a seafood or light tomato sauce (e.g. *linguine* with clams) or creamy sauces (*spaghetti carbonara*) or with pesto. *Gnocchi*. *Risotto*. Seafood salad. Chargrilled squid. *Fritto misto*.

Vinho Verde and other Portuguese whites Grilled or barbecued sardines. Other oily fish.

SMOOTH, MED-BODIED DRY WHITES

General Salmon. Fish, chicken, pork or veal with creamy sauces. Roast or grilled chicken. Chicken pie. Escalopes of chicken or veal. Egg-based dishes such as omelettes, quiches or souffles. Creamy pasta dishes.

Alsace Pinot Blanc *Quiche Lorraine*.

Burgundy Plainly cooked (e.g. poached) salmon, Dover sole, turbot. Langoustines. Roast turkey.

Chardonnay and Chardonnay blends Lighter more citrussy styles: cooked fish dishes such as fish cakes, fish pies, seared scallops. Sweeter, fruitier styles such as **Sémillon-Chardonnay**: spicy chicken and pork dishes.

Chenin Blanc *See* lighter styles of Chardonnay.

Colombard *See* Sémillon-Chardonnay.

RICH, FULL-BODIED WHITES

General Classic *haute cuisine*. Richly flavoured chicken, fish and shellfish. Buttery sauces.

Chardonnay European style (Burgundian, Californian): rich lobster and shellfish dishes, fine white fish such as halibut and turbot. New World style (Australian): robustly flavoured or spiced chicken, pork and fish dishes. Steak if you enjoy a white wine with it.

Marsanne (Australian) *See* Sémillon.

Pessac-Léognan/Graves *See* European style Chardonnay.

Sémillon Full-flavoured chicken and pork dishes. Southeast Asian/Pacific Rim cuisine.

AROMATIC & MEDIUM-DRY WHITES

General Hard to generalise because this category encompasses so many contrasting styles. Most aromatic wines have some affinity with creamy sauces and with slightly spicy food.

Gewürztraminer Smoked meats and fish (including smoked salmon), Chinese (Cantonese) food, milder curries, pungent cheeses (especially Munster).

Riesling German Kabinett: Light fish and meat dishes. Salmon and trout (particularly with a creamy sauce). Smoked meats, salads, lightly seasoned stir fries. *Choucroute*. Spätlese: duck, goose. Alsace: similar to German Riesling but can take slightly richer flavours. Australian: excellent with Thai and Pacific Rim style food.

Tokay-Pinot Gris Rich poultry and pork dishes. Guineafowl.

Viognier Light and slightly spicy chicken and veal.

Vouvray and other medium-dry whites Chicken or pork dishes with creamy, slightly sweet sauces or in dishes which incorporate fruit, like pineapple, apricots and prunes.

LIGHT, FRUITY REDS

General A wide range of cold and cured meats, simply grilled chicken, pork and veal. Robustly seasoned and barbecued fish dishes. Mediterranean style food, stuffed vegetables.

Beaujolais *Charcuterie*. Cold roast ham (and boiled or grilled gammon). Creamy, soft rind cheeses like Brie and Camembert.

Côtes du Rhône Simple chicken and pork dishes.

Chinon and other Loire reds Similar to Beaujolais. Also good with goat's cheese

Pinot Noir Burgundy (lighter styles): snails in garlic butter, roast duck, pheasant, partridge. New World: seared and chargrilled meat and fish.

Tempranillo Pork with olives, barbecued chicken and pork.

Valpolicella and other Italian reds Most types of pasta (except those with creamy and seafood sauces). Pizza, Italian-style sausages.

SMOOTH, MEDIUM-BODIED REDS

General Most types of meat, especially plainly cooked beef and lamb and homely dishes like shepherds pie and sausages.

Beaujolais cru Duck, rabbit, roast or braised veal.

Bordeaux Roast beef and lamb, lighter stews and casseroles, omelettes (for more traditional styles), hard cheeses.

Burgundy Roast game, venison, kidneys, *coq au vin*, *boeuf bourguignonne*, dishes containing mushrooms, soft rind cheeses.

Chianti and other Italian reds Grilled and roast pork, calves liver, richer pasta dishes like *canneloni* and *lasagne*.

Merlot (New World style) Chargrilled meat and vegetables.

Rioja, Navarra Grilled lamb, particularly with herbs, hard cheeses.

FULL-BODIED REDS

General Chargrilled steaks, casseroles, spicy meat and vegetarian dishes such as *goulash*.

Barbaresco and Barolo Rich meat and game, especially hare. Mushrooms and truffles.

Cabernet Sauvignon European style: beef, venison with rich sauces, chargrilled lamb. New World style (Australia, Chile): *chilli con carne*, hotter types of Indian food.

Fitou and other southern French reds Cassoulet, duck confit, lamb with flageolets.

Hermitage (Rhône reds) Big braises and *daubes*.

Shiraz Barbecued meat, kangaroo.

Zinfandel Oxtail, chilli dishes, barbecued ribs.

AGED REDS & RARITIES

Aged reds Older versions of classic wines like Bordeaux, Burgundy and Rioja will go with similar types of dishes to more recent vintages but keep the food simple. Older wines go particularly well with game.

Rarities Take a similar approach to older wines. Keep the food simple.

Amarone Richly sauced meat and game.

Salice Salentino and other southern Italian reds Robustly cooked meat and vegetable dishes, aubergines, hard cheeses.

ROSES

General Similar dishes to crisp, dry whites. Milder curries and other lightly spiced dishes.

Bandol and other Provence rosés Typically Mediterranean dishes such as *aioli, salade niçoise, bouillabaisse, ratatouille*.

Bordeaux rosé Elegant summery fish and chicken.

New World rosé Pacific Rim cuisine, barbecues.

Rosado (Spanish rosé) *Paella*, couscous.

Rosé d'Anjou and other medium-dry rosés Chicken or prawn salads.

Tavel Similar to Provence rosés. Fish soup.

CHAMPAGNE & SPARKLING WINES

General Lighter styles go with similar food to crisp, dry whites. Fuller styles, with the same type of food as good quality white burgundy.

Lighter styles (NV, blanc de blancs) *Canapés*, caviar, smoked salmon, *sushi*, shellfish, scrambled eggs, Chinese (Cantonese) food.

Richer, toastier styles (vintage, prestige cuvées, quality New World sparkling wines) Richly sauced seafood and shellfish. Lightly sauced chicken and pork dishes.

Demi-Sec Lightly spiced dishes. Creamy sauces.

Sweet Light fruit-based desserts. Fruit salad, mousses, meringues and lemon desserts go well with sweet Italian sparklers such as Asti.

Rose Lightly spiced Chinese and Southeast Asian food. Richer wines can be drunk with rare lamb, pork and plainly cooked game birds.

Red New World cooking, barbecues.

SWEET WINES

General Fruit-based and creamy puddings are the easiest to match, chocolate the trickiest. The wine should be sweeter than the pudding. Try lighter sweet wines with creamy blue cheeses.

Australian Liqueur Muscat Pecan pie, walnut tart, mince pies, coffee cake, vanilla ice-cream.

Beerenauslese and other German and Austrian sweet wines Simple fruit tarts.

Late Harvest Riesling and Sémillon (New World) Exotic fruit salads, Southeast Asian influenced desserts.

Mavrodaphne of Patras and other sweet red wines Red fruits, pears in red wine, dark chocolate cake and puddings.

Muscat de Beaumes de Venise and other southern French Muscats Strawberries and cream, fruit tarts, crumbles, Christmas pudding.

Moscatel de Valencia Citrus based desserts e.g. oranges in caramel, *crèpes suzette*, trifle.

Orange Muscat Fruit salads, orange flavoured puddings, dark chocolate.

Sauternes and other sweet Bordeaux *Foie gras*, fruit tarts, *crème brûlée*, traditional British puddings. Roquefort.

Tokay *Tarte Tatin*, treacle tart.

Vendange Tardive (Alsace) *Foie gras*, fruit tarts.

Vouvray and other sweet Loire wines Pear and apple tarts or flans.

FORTIFIED WINES

Amontillado and dry oloroso sherry; Bual and Verdelho Madeira An alternative to port with cheese. Nut tarts. Turron.

Banyuls, Rivesaltes and other vins doux naturels Chocolate desserts, desserts with prunes. Christmas pudding.

Fino and manzanilla sherry; Sercial Madeira; white port As an aperitif with olives and nuts, *chorizo* sausage, *tortilla* and other *tapas*. With classic soups such as *consommé*.

Marsala *Zabaglione*, almond cake.

Ruby port styles (Late Bottled Vintage, Vintage Character) Chocolate cake. Cheese.

Sweet oloroso sherry; Malmsey Madeira Baked apples. Christmas cake and pudding, vanilla ice cream.

Tawny port styles Hard cheeses. Christmas cake. Walnut tart.

Vintage port Stilton and other traditional British and Irish cheeses.

STORING AND SERVING WINE

Few people, if you asked them, would think they had anything to do with the way a wine tastes. They imagine that once the wine is bottled that, like a can of beans, it continues to taste the same way until you open it. But, in fact, the way you store a wine, and the way you choose to serve it, has a marked effect on the way it ends up in the glass.

Storing wine

Unless you drink a bottle of wine within a month or two of bringing it home, it may start to change its character. Whether or not that's a good thing depends on the type of wine and your own taste. A young, crisp white loses its freshness quite rapidly and certainly won't improve from being kept for more than a few weeks. A full-bodied red, on the other hand, may well benefit from being laid down in a cool dark place for a year or so giving a chance for more complex mellow flavours to develop.

The problem is that you don't always know how old a wine is when you buy it. At one extreme it may be just a few weeks old. Wineries these days are under considerable pressure to release their wines as quickly as possible (the sooner they do, the sooner they get paid) so the wine can in fact still be in a state of "bottle shock" and may actually improve from being allowed to lie down quietly for a few weeks. For this reason it is best to avoid a wine a shop proudly announces has just arrived unless you are prepared to give it a rest.

At the other extreme are wines that may have been hanging around on a shelf or in a restaurant cellar for several months. Hot bright lights can be particularly damaging, so it's best to avoid a bottle that has been sitting under a spotlight, particularly if it actually feels warm to the touch. Shops will often sell off stock that is near the end of its shelf life as a "bin end" which can be a good deal provided you drink it straight away. As a rule of thumb, if the wine seems too old for its style (*see* below), don't attempt to store it for any length of time yourself.

Most inexpensive and medium-priced wines are, in fact, designed to be drunk more or less immediately, so it's not worth buying more than you're likely to need for the next couple of months. Storage becomes more of an issue with better quality white and red wines, particularly those from Bordeaux and Burgundy that are only affordable if you buy them when they're first released.

The temptation always with reds is to keep them too long (the theory being that if they're older they must be better) but in my experience, it's far more common to be disappointed by a bottle that's been kept for too long, than one that's been opened too soon. Only a small handful of very expensive wines, like top German Rieslings, sweet Loire whites and big, full-bodied Rhône reds that can be impossibly tough and tannic in their youth, repay extended cellaring.

Storage options

Unfortunately, few of us have houses with cellars, but that doesn't mean there aren't other places which are perfectly good for storing wine. What's good about a cellar is that it is cool, dark and damp, so wine remains at a constant temperature and corks don't dry out.

What wine doesn't like is warmth, vibration and wildly fluctuating temperatures. Unsuitable places include areas like uninsulated garages or outside buildings which get very hot in summer and cold in winter (lighter wines will freeze if the temperature actually drops much below freezing) or, as many people do in fact store it, in a bright warm kitchen on top of a fridge or next to a boiler.

If you have no more than a couple of cases, the best place to put them is in a cupboard in a spare bedroom, or under the stairs at a temperature that doesn't exceed 20˚C or drop below 10˚C. You need to take care that it's free from extraneous smells such as chemicals, paint or cleaning products, that the bottles are stored on their side so that the wine is in touch with the cork and air can't seep into the bottle. You also need a reasonable degree of humidity (this can be achieved simply by putting a bowl of water on the floor).

If you are serious about collecting wine, you can buy temperature-controlled cabinets or even have a purpose-built spiral cellar installed, but unless you are nursing a particularly valuable collection, it is a substantial investment to make. It may, in fact, be more practical to get the company you buy the wine from to store it for you, though you should only do this if you are dealing with a reputable and well-established dealer. While it does mean your wine is likely to be stored in near-perfect conditions, it does of course have the drawback that you can't pull out a bottle when the mood takes you.

Serving

There's a lot of off-putting mystique surrounding the serving of wine which is actually a great deal less complicated than it sometimes sounds. Nevertheless, it is true that you can actually make wine taste better if you give a little bit of care and attention to the way you serve it.

Above *A temperature-controlled cabinet such as this – just like a fridge but specially designed for wine – is ideal for homes with limited cellaring facilities.*

Far left *A traditional underground cellar, for those fortunate enough to have one, is the ideal choice for long-term personal wine storage.*

Temperature

The thing that will make the biggest difference to your enjoyment of a glass of wine is the temperature at which you serve it. The conventional wisdom is that whites should be served chilled, and reds at room temperature, but that begs the question of how cold your fridge is or how warm a room you leave it in. These days, with rooms regularly heated to at least 20°C, there's a danger that if you leave a red wine out too long it will get unpleasantly soupy. Most reds, in fact, are better for being left in a relatively cool place before serving, with light, fruity reds, like Beaujolais, even benefiting from an hour in the fridge.

With whites there tends to be the opposite danger of chilling them too much which can dull their aroma and flavour. While light, crisp whites, aromatic whites and sweet and sparkling wines benefit from being quite cold (at least an hour in the average fridge), richer, fuller-bodied whites can be served a little warmer (chill them for no more than an hour). If you are served a glass of wine that is too cold you can warm it up by cupping your hands round the glass.

Changing the temperature quickly

If you are caught unprepared you can chill a wine quickly by plunging the bottle into a bucket of iced water (quicker than just ice) or by popping it in the freezer for 20 minutes (though don't whatever you do forget that you've put it there). You can now also buy insulated "jackets" which you keep in the freezer and slip over the bottle as needed. If you need to warm up a wine slightly (for instance, a full-bodied red that has been kept in an unheated room) place the bottle in a bowl or bucket of warm water.

Pulling the cork

There's a general idea that you need to open a bottle of red wine at least an hour in advance of drinking it. In fact, the act of pulling the cork doesn't benefit the wine hugely if you don't pour anything out of the bottle. The point about opening a wine in advance (other than to check it's not corked) is to get air into it in order to open up the flavours. Traditionally, that used to be done with reds that were likely to be tough or tannic, but the majority of wines these days, don't really need opening up in this way. If you do have a wine that you think can benefit from aerating and that can include full-bodied whites as well as particularly robust full-bodied reds, you might just as well decant it.

Decanting

The whole idea of decanting makes people nervous. In fact, it's nothing more than pouring wine from one container to another, exposing it to the air and helping to release its aromas. To do this, simply transfer it straight into a clean jug or decanter. (If you use a jug, you can follow the sommeliers' trick of pouring the wine over the back of a spoon to give it maximum exposure to the air. If you don't want to have a jug on the table just pour the wine carefully back into the bottle again.)

The other reason to decant is because the wine has accumulated a heavy deposit or sediment that you don't want to end up in your glass. If you're dealing with this kind of wine (or port) leave the bottle upright for at least 24 hours (preferably for a couple of days), then, with a light placed behind the bottle (a lamp or a torch will do), steadily pour the wine, stopping when the sediment reaches the neck of the bottle. It is not difficult, simply a matter of having a watchful eye and a steady hand.

There are wines that do not benefit from decanting, particularly fine old red wines whose fragile aromas and complex flavours can rapidly evaporate once exposed to the air. Another wine, ironically, is dry sherry which rapidly loses its fresh, tangy character if stored, as frequently used to be the case, in a decanter.

Glasses

People tend to choose glasses more for their looks than for their suitability for drinking wine but the shape and thickness of a glass can have a marked effect on flavour. The problem with the basic "Paris goblet" type of wine glass is that it's too small and delivers the wine in a rush, so that you've barely tasted it before swallowing it.

What you need is a plain, clear glass with a generously sized bowl that slightly tapers towards the rim so you can swirl the wine around to release and enjoy its aromas. The stem of the glass should be long enough so that you don't have to hold it by the bowl (otherwise the heat of your hand will warm the wine) and it should have a fine thin rim which makes it easier to sip and savour the wine rather than just gulp it down. As a counsel of perfection, you would have a different type of glass for each type of wine. In fact, there is an Austrian glass designer, Georg Riedel, who has produced just that and there's no doubt that the right shaped glass enhances the varietal character and style of a particular wine. But given that not many of us can afford a wardrobe of different glasses, a more realistic target would be a largeish wineglass of the type

Above *The intriguing sight of a wine glass being blown. The quality and shape of wine glasses can have a surprising influence on the appreciation of a wine's aromas and flavours.*

Far left *When decanting wine, hold the bottle over a flame or a pocket torch to see when the sediment reaches the neck of the bottle. This is when to stop pouring.*

I've described above for full-bodied white and most red wines, a slightly smaller wine glass for more aromatic white wines and light reds, a small "copita" type sherry glass which would also double for port and dessert wines and a tall champagne "flute". If you can only afford one of these extras I would go for the flute. It traps the champagne bubbles and aromas far more effectively than the traditional saucer shaped glass.

Keeping glasses clean

It is also important that your glasses, whatever their shape, should be scrupulously clean. Grease, dust and detergent residues can all affect the taste of your wine. The most efficient way to wash your glasses is to run them through a dishwasher without any detergent, though repeated use can scratch fine glasses. Personally, I think it's better to wash them as soon as possible in the hottest water you can bear, rinse them and dry them immediately with a clean linen tea towel. Either way you should store them upright rather than upended or you'll trap any stale air.

Pouring

When you're pouring wine you should only fill the glass half to two-thirds full. The problem is that this may be misinterpreted as lack of generosity but if you want to enjoy a wine's aromas, which are half the pleasure of tasting, you need to leave room to swirl it around.

Order of serving

Without being unnecessarily hidebound about it, it does make sense to follow the conventional serving order for most wines. In just the way that you wouldn't serve a robust casserole before a light fish dish, or a pudding before your main course, so it makes sense to serve a light wine before a powerfully concentrated one and a dry wine before a sweet one. There is, however, no reason why you shouldn't serve a light red before a rich, full-bodied white: weight is more important than colour.

Leftovers

After the first hour or two, the exposure to air that was so beneficial on first opening the bottle starts reacting adversely on the wine and will eventually turn it to vinegar. So, if you have half a bottle or less left over try and decant it into a smaller bottle, recork it, then pop it into the fridge. (It's well worth keeping one or two half bottles for this purpose.)

There are also wine preservation systems which pump air out of the bottle or ones that pump in a layer of inert gas. Some people swear by them but, to be honest, I don't think they're a great deal better than a cork – maybe because wine is never lying around our house for that long. Surprisingly, champagne does keep its fizz if it's left in the fridge overnight if you put an upended teaspoon in the bottle. Dessert wines will keep longer than most table wines as will most types of port and sherry (except fino and manzanilla which should be treated like white wine). But that doesn't mean you should keep them for years.

Wine faults

There are certain quirky characteristics of particular types of wine that you can imagine are faults if you haven't come across them before. The coarse boiled asparagus-like smell of Sauvignon Blanc which is sometimes rudely compared to cat's pee, the odd, slightly petrolly smell of mature Riesling, the rank farmyardy aromas of aged burgundy, although sometimes unappetising, are within the normal range of aromas and flavours that can be expected from these wines. But if you encounter any of the following aromas (in most cases you don't actually have to taste a wine to tell that it's faulty) you can safely assume something is seriously wrong:

- A musty, mouldy, dank smell. If it's just a faint trace it may be what's called "bottle stink" – a pocket of stale air trapped in the bottle which will clear within about 10 to 15 minutes of opening. If it doesn't or the smell is more pronounced it's more likely that the cork is contaminated, i.e. that the wine is "corked".
- White wine with slightly brackish, sherried smell, usually combined with a dark yellow colour is likely to be oxidised and therefore well past its best.
- A strong smell of bad eggs or drains. This indicates an excess of sulphur in the wine.
- A thin, very sharp wine. Everyone's tolerance of acid in wine varies, but if it's mouthpuckeringly sour, it shouldn't be.
- A stewed, baked, slightly flabby character in reds usually means the fermentation temperature has been allowed to rise too high and the wine is over-extracted. Not undrinkable, but unacceptable.

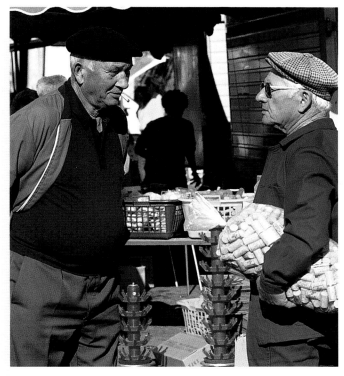

Above *Stopping for a quick chat at the cork market in the Beaujolais region in France.*

Far left *The cork oak unlike other trees, allows its thick spongey bark to be stripped off without the rest of the tree being harmed. The quality of the cork is crucial – if it is contaminated, it can cause faulty or "corked" wines which will smell dank or musty. This faulty wine (right) should be a pale golden yellow, but, because too much air has got in through the cork (oxidation), it is now an unattractive dull, dark yellow.*

INDEX

Indexer's note: Grape varieties and wines made from the same varieties are indexed together, as are places or vineyards and wines named after them.

ACKNOWLEDGMENTS

The author's name may be on the jacket but books are basically a team effort. So thanks first and foremost to my fellow members of the editorial team – to Sue Jamieson whose idea the book originally was, to Margaret Little who saw the project through so skillfully, to Lucy Bridgers without whose respect for deadlines it might never have been delivered and to Fiona Knowles who was responsible for the incredibly stylish and eye-catching design.

I also relied heavily on many friends and colleagues in the wine trade who gave their help unstintingly and generously: among them Charlotte Hey of Wines from Spain, Emma Roberts of SOPEXA, Fiona Morrison of the CIVB (for her help on Bordeaux) and Jasper Morris of Morris & Verdin (for his on Burgundy), and Liz Robertson of Safeway, Hugh Suter of Bibendum, Meg Brodman of Cellarworld and Alastair Mayling of International Wine Services for revealing the intricacies of the winemaker's art.

Finally – and not least – a big thank you to my family: to my husband Trevor who first introduced me to the pleasure of good wine and who together with my children William, Jordan, Kate and Flyn survived four months of an excessively preoccupied wife and mother with heroic patience and good humour.

t = top; b = bottom; c = centre

Cephas Picture Library/Mick Rock 33, 114. **Corbis UK Ltd/Morton Beebe** 83. **Patrick Eagar** 16, 17, 19, 79. **Armin Faber** 26, 29. **Getty Images Ltd./The Tony Stone Collection** 86, 100, 104, 105. **Robert Harding Picture Library** 113t/**Liaison Int.** 110. **Image Bank/Michael Melford** 30. **Brian Jordan** 36. **Reed Consumer Books Limited/James Johnson** 8, 9, 111b/**Ray Moller** 33b/**Steven Morris** 11b, 37b, 39b, 41b, 43b, 45b, 47b, 49b, 51 b, 53 b, 55 b, 57b, 59b, 61b, 63b, 65b, 67b, 69b, 71b, 73b, 75b, 77b, 79b, 81b, 83b, 85b, 87b, 89b, 91b, 93b, 95b, 97b, 99b, 101b, 103 b, 105b, 113 b, 113 c 115 b. **Janet Price** 13, 15, 21, 23, 37, 42, 55. **Root Stock/Tessa van der Haar** 24/**Hendrik Holler** 10, 11, 12, 14, 18, 22, 28, 32, 43, 48. 49, 54, 66, 67, 72, 93, 98. **Scope/Jean- Luc Barde** 60, 111t, 115t/ **Bernard Galeron** 61/**Philip Gould** 20/**Jacques Guillard** 73, 82, 87t/**Michel Guillard** 25, 27, 78, 92, 112/**Noel Hautemaniere** 102/**Francis Jalain** 31. Author photography: **Ian Cook**

The author and publishers would also like to thank:
Oddbins Ltd for supplying the wines for photography.
Michael Johnson (Ceramics) Ltd for the loan of Riedel wine glasses.